THE
DORSET & SOMERSET CANAL

INLAND WATERWAYS HISTORIES
Edited by Charles Hadfield

The Dorset & Somerset Canal. By Kenneth R. Clew
The Kennet & Avon Canal. By Kenneth R. Clew
London's Lost Route to Basingstoke. By P. A. L. Vine
London's Lost Route to the Sea. By P. A. L. Vine
The Nutbrook Canal: Derbyshire. By Peter Stevenson
The Somersetshire Coal Canal and Railways. By Kenneth R. Clew
The Thames & Severn Canal. By Humphrey Household
The Yorkshire Ouse. By Baron F. Duckham

in preparation
The Bude Canal. By H. Harris and M. Ellis
The Exeter Canal. By Kenneth R. Clew
The Forth & Clyde Canal. By Graham Matheson and D. Light
The Grand Junction Canal. By Alan H. Faulkner
The Great Ouse. By D. Summers
The Leicester Line. By Philip A. Stevens
The Royal Military Canal. By P. A. L. Vine
The Stroudwater Navigation. By M. A. Handford

THE
DORSET & SOMERSET CANAL

An Illustrated History

by

KENNETH R. CLEW

With 8 plates and 10 text illustrations
including maps

and a foreword by
PETER PAGAN, BA, FLA, AMBIM
(*Director, Bath Municipal Libraries
& Victoria Art Gallery*)

DAVID & CHARLES: NEWTON ABBOT

ISBN 0 7153 5228 8

Set in 11 pt Garamond, 2 pt leaded
and printed in Great Britain
by Latimer Trend & Company Limited Plymouth
for David & Charles (Publishers) Limited
South Devon House Newton Abbot Devon

TO JEAN

Contents

Illustrations

MAPS

Foreword

'WATER is best,' says the Greek adage carved (*inter alios locos*) above the portals of the Pump Room at Bath. In the eager search for a new, safe, and above all reliable means of conveyance for the products of the new industrial revolution, and for the bulky raw materials which were being consumed in ever-increasing quantities, the long immutable stretches of placid level water, immune from sudden hills and valleys, and the upsets of steep banks and pothole ditches trapping the unwary wheel, had an immediate appeal. On these ribbons of confined water would be gently and inexorably borne, with the minimum of effort, the largest and heaviest loads that commerce could conceive.

The practical problems were, it was reported, not difficult to surmount, thanks to the new found ingenuity of the engineers. And the capital costs would, all being well, see a rich return, in dues and carriage charges; the projects were, potentially, economically viable. A flourishing canal would be a highway to the sea, partaking of the nature of the sea (which island Englishmen so well understood), and yet free from tides and shoals and sudden foul weather.

This is the field which Ken Clew has explored. The gentle persuasion of management meetings and financial provision; the genteel arguments, hopes and fears; the squabbles; the dreams—and the non-reality. Of the diggers themselves, whether the rumbustious 'navigators' who dug and brawled and swore and sweated their way across the canal maps of

England: or the local labour, recruited for a specific length, and with their roots in the countryside through which the waterway was passing, there are only faint but fascinating glimpses and echoes. The 'policy decisions'—diversions to meet the real or imagined fears of the landowners; struggles to keep to deadlines; anxious assessments of new methods and inventions which might offer a cheaper solution—and all the time the ever mounting costs: these are the things that were recorded, minuted, and discussed in correspondence. And this is the author's source material for the history of the canal.

Work ceased—the dream collapsed—over 160 years ago. More than a few traces still remain to be sought and discovered. Here is the background and guide, an overall view and conspectus of the heyday of the work, lovingly and carefully reconstructed by a master in the art of such discovery.

PETER PAGAN

Preface

ONE bomb fell on Wincanton during the last war and destroyed almost all known records of the Dorset & Somerset Canal. If completed, the canal would have had a major effect upon the economy of rural Dorset, forming a link with both Poole and Bristol. This was not to be, though there is still a story to tell of the hopes and frustrations of its company of proprietors.

With the generous help and encouragement of Robin Atthill, Charles Hadfield and many other friends, I have tried to piece this story together with the aid of early newspapers and other contemporary records. It has been a rewarding task to unearth the history of the D & S and I hope that it will give pleasure to many others.

KENNETH R. CLEW

Gillumsfield
April 1970

A Canal from Bristol
to Poole, 1793

THERE was madness in the air towards the end of the eighteenth century. The King, George III, had suffered his first serious bout of what was then thought to be insanity, whilst across the Channel the horrors of the French Revolutionary Wars were being experienced. At home there was a different kind of madness—*Canal Mania*.

The success of the early waterways such as the Duke of Bridgewater's Canal from Worsley collieries to Manchester, the Birmingham Canal, the Staffordshire & Worcestershire and Trent & Mersey had encouraged a multiplicity of new schemes. Many were subsequently seen to be futile propositions once a preliminary survey had been undertaken, but this in no way deterred the numbers of speculators wishing to invest in canal shares.

By the end of 1792 the Canal Mania reached Bristol. A promotion meeting was held on 20 November for a Bristol & Severn Canal between Bristol and Gloucester 'or some other more convenient place' and was

> enthusiastically supported by influential persons, and a large sum subscribed by those present, who struggled violently with each other in their rush to the subscription book.[1]

Although the Bristol & Severn scheme was abandoned in 1797, others were more successful, including the revival of a scheme to link the rivers Avon and Kennet. This project, the Western

Canal (later to be renamed the Kennet & Avon Canal) was completed in 1810.

The boom in canal shares continued throughout the early part of 1793, despite the warning note sounded in a Bristol newspaper:[2]

> The different Canal Meetings that have lately proved abortive may be a means of preventing the public from following every *ignis fatuus* held up to their view . . .

Even so, some six months later, in September 1793 there were no fewer than twenty advertisements for canals in the *Bristol Gazette*.[3] Amongst them was one for the Dorset and Somerset Inland Navigation.

The D & S began as the result of a meeting at the Bear Inn, Wincanton on 10 January 1793, held 'for the purpose of taking into consideration the propriety of an Inland Communication between Poole and Bristol'.[4] Such a canal would provide a link between the English and Bristol Channels and avoid the long and hazardous passage around the coasts of Land's End. The idea of a link between the two channels was not a new one for as early as 1769 Robert Whitworth, a pupil of James Brindley, had surveyed the route for a proposed Exeter & Uphill Canal to join the South Devon and Somerset coasts.

Though nothing came of the Exeter & Uphill Canal project, the new scheme had far more chance of success. The Wincanton meeting was told that the D & S could depend on two certain commodities for trade—coal and potter's clay. Coal from the Bristol and Somerset coalfields was carried to most parts of Dorset by land carriage at a considerable expense, whilst potter's clay for the Potteries district of Staffordshire had to travel from the Wareham area by coastal vessel to Bristol. If the D & S was cut as planned there would be a regular trade throughout the line of navigation in both directions in coal and clay alone, in addition to subsidary trades such as barley, etc.

Those present agreed that the D & S would be 'of the greatest Publick utility' and that the line of the canal should follow, as far as was practicable, a route from Bath to Frome (with a branch

from Frome to the Mendip collieries), thence by way of Wincanton, Henstridge, Stalbridge, Sturminster Newton, Lydlinch,
Kingstag bridge, Mappowder, Ansty, Puddletown, and Wareham to Poole Harbour. It was decided to hold a further meeting
at the Bear Inn, Wincanton, on 7 February (this being considered the most central place), so that the landowners who
would be affected could attend 'to consider of the above
Resolutions' and subscribe for shares.

Shares were to be limited to a maximum of five per person,
each to be of £100 in value and, apart from those attending the
first meeting, subscriptions would be restricted to the landowners through whose property the canal was intended to pass,
and to the inhabitants of those parishes to avoid any 'improper
speculation'. A deposit of £1 1s (£1·05) per cent was to be
paid on each share to Messrs Whitmash, Messiter & Luff,
bankers of Wincanton, towards defraying the preliminary
expenses.

The bankers had another connection with the canal because
one of the partners, Richard Messiter, was appointed secretary
of the Wincanton meeting. Richard Messiter was a lawyer by
profession and had succeeded his father as under-sheriff of
Somerset and later, in 1787, was elected treasurer for the
eastern division of the county. He pioneered many improve-
ments in the Wincanton area, clothed and armed troops of the
volunteer infantry, established the Horwood well as a minor
spa and generally benefited the neighbourhood by his activi-
ties.[5] He was the eldest of six sons; three others, John, Uriah
and George, and one of his seven sisters, Letitia, also being
concerned with the D & S as officials or shareholders.[6]

The various resolutions approved at the Wincanton meeting
were ordered by the chairman, John Berkeley Burland, to be
published in the Bath, Bristol, Salisbury and Sherborne newspapers. The editorial comment of the *Bath Chronicle* was terse:
'The great advantages of this canal are set forth in this advertisement.'[7]

Soon afterwards, on 26 January, a meeting of the corpora-

B

tion and inhabitants of the Borough of Wareham took place at their Town Hall 'for the purpose of taking into consideration, the propriety of the proposed inland Communication between Bristol and Poole'.[8] The Mayor, I. Lawrence, was in the chair and the Town Clerk, T. Bartlett jun, secretary to the meeting. It was resolved,

> that we will give every support and alliance in our power, to the plan and Resolutions proposed, and resolved at the Wincanton Meeting.
>
> That the Members for the County, the Members for this Borough, and such other Members of Parliament as the Committee to be appointed at this Meeting shall think proper to apply to, be requested to give their support in Parliament to the Bill for such Canal by the course and line before proposed.[9]

The committee appointed consisted of the following gentlemen: John Calcraft, Nathanial Bond, Jonathan Lawrence, John Dampier, Thomas Bartlett, Thomas Brown, Giles Brown, Rev Brice, Rev Jones, Rev Colson, Messrs Filliter, Bartlett jun, Thomas Phippard, Thomas Garland, Richard Wright, John Card, William Cole and John Wills. Committee meetings were to be open to 'any gentlemen of the town and neighbourhood, who may think it proper to attend'. It was also decided that subscriptions, to defray expenses, be immediately commenced.

Another meeting, this time of the landowners and inhabitants of the eastern parts of Dorset, was held two days later at the Crown Inn, Blandford Forum. The fulsome support given to the proposals by the inhabitants of Wareham was not endorsed by those present at Blandford Forum, who considered that the canal would be of more benefit to the county and more productive to the proprietors if the route, from Sturminster Newton, was altered to run by way of Blandford and Wimborne to Poole.

A committee of twelve was appointed to arrange for a survey of the proposed alteration between Sturminster Newton and Poole, so that a plan and estimates of the expense could be prepared. John Frankland, chairman of this meeting, was on the committee as also were Thomas Street, Thomas Bastard, William Spurrier jun, Samuel White jun, George Sibley, Rupert Oke, Joseph Bird, John Davis, William Clapcott, Richard Allen and George Edward Huffey. They were asked to contact John Berkeley Burland, chairman of the Wincanton committee, to inform him of the resolutions passed at the Blandford meeting,

> and also to attend the meeting to be held at Wincanton on the 7th of February next, and to represent at the said meeting the probable advantages attending the above-mentioned direction of the said canal; and to request that all further proceedings on the said business might be suspended 'till the survey and plan proposed at this meeting be prepared.[10]

Meanwhile, yet another route for the canal south of Sturminster Newton was under discussion. All that is known of this proposal is an advertisement, headed 'DORSET CANAL by ALTON', in the *Sherborne Mercury*.[11]

> . . . it being the opinion of many respectable landholders and other inhabitants of the eastern parts of the county, that an improvement may be made in the route of the said canal, an experienced person is now taking the different elevations of the ground from King's Stag Bridge to Aller, and from the same points to Alton Pancras, in order to ascertain the most practicable approach from the Vale of Blackmore to Piddle Town and Wareham.

The plans would be produced at a meeting to be held at the New Inn, Cerne Abbas, on Tuesday, 5 February, when all interested persons were requested to attend.

It is probable that the Cerne Abbas meeting was organised by some of the landowners who would be affected by the construction of the canal through their properties, for the route now proposed would follow the course of the river Piddle from Puddletown to Wareham. In case this did not meet with general approval, it was suggested that a cut could be made from Puddletown to join with the river Frome and so lead to

Wareham 'without interfering with the parks or pleasure grounds of any gentleman whatever'.

Neither suggestion appears to have found favour because, a fortnight later, another advertisement was placed in the *Sherborne Mercury*[12] to propose that a canal from Ilchester to Poole by way of Yeovil, Cerne Abbas, Dorchester and Wareham would be of greater value than the D & S. Such canal would join with the Bristol & Western Canal below Langport and so provide a through route to the Grand Western Canal. It noted that the river Yeo was already navigable from Langport to Load bridge, about 1 mile from Ilchester, and that the distance from the latter town to Wareham was only about 40 miles.

One sentence in the advertisement leads to the conclusion that the organisers of the Cerne Abbas meeting were also responsible for this latest scheme. The sentence in question follows a summary of the advantages and ends with the significant words 'by the track proposed, it would not interfere with the parks or pleasure grounds of any gentleman whatever'— an almost identical phrase to that used in the advertisement for the Cerne Abbas meeting.

The Ilchester to Poole Canal scheme was never completed as planned though, in 1794, part of its route between Langport and Ilchester was surveyed for an improved navigation of the river Yeo. An Act was obtained in 1795[13] for the Ivelchester & Langport Navigation and work began almost at once on the 8¼ mile long line. By 1797 rising costs had exhausted all money raised and there was little hope of obtaining the sum required to complete the works, because of the inflationary effects of the French Revolutionary Wars. Consequently the shareholders decided to leave the navigation uncompleted until times were easier. The river Yeo was still usable in its unimproved state, but the Ivelchester & Langport Navigation was never finished.

Similarly, the Bristol & Western Canal scheme also failed, though this was eventually revived and partially completed as the Bridgwater & Taunton Canal in 1827. The Grand Western Canal did not live up to its expectations either, and all that was

cut of a canal authorised to run between Taunton and Topsham
was the 24½ miles from Taunton to Tiverton.

In contrast to the apparent lack of response to the Cerne
Abbas meeting on 5 February, 'a very respectable and numerous meeting'[14] of the proprietors of lands affected by the D & S
was held at the Bear Inn, Wincanton, on Thursday, 7 February
1793. There was unanimous approval of the resolution that a
canal between Bristol and Poole would be of great advantage
to both the commercial and landed interests of the country.

As two different lines for the D & S had been proposed, a long
debate followed about the merits of the route south of Stalbridge via Bagber (with a communication to Sturminster Newton), Kingstag bridge, Plush, Piddletrenthide and Puddletown
to Wareham, compared with that via Sturminster Newton,
Blandford and Wimborne to Poole. Evidently the views of
John Frankland and his committee from Blandford Forum
were considered seriously, because a final decision on the route
was deferred, it being resolved:

> That before any positive determination respecting the line of
> the Canal be fixed on, some eminent surveyor or surveyors,
> engineers or other persons, be appointed to take the necessary
> levels and make proper calculations and estimates of the ex-
> pences likely to be incurred, as well as of the tonnage likely to
> arise on the lines respectively proposed, and to report the same
> to a committee to be appointed by this meeting. . . .[15]

The choice of the committee was a masterly compromise
between the various factions of Wincanton, Wareham and
Blandford. The members elected were: The Earl of Ilchester,
Samuel Bailward, Peter Sherston, Harry Edgell, John Billings-
ley, Samuel Kelston, Thomas Davis, William Toogood,
Edmund Ogden, Rev John Toogood, Rev Harry Place, Rev
William Bishop, George Filliter, Thomas Bartlett jun, John
Frankland, John Lester, Francis Webb, Robert James, Thomas
Street and William Clapcott. The Rev Samuel Farewell, Vicar
of Wincanton, was also concerned as he acted as chairman at
this and some later meetings of the committee.

Any seven or more members were empowered to act on behalf of the whole committee. In view of the numerous opinions and interests represented, there was no danger that any one faction would be able to hold sway over the others. Messrs Thomas Bartlett jun and George Filliter had previously been on the committee elected at the Wareham meeting, similarly John Frankland and William Clapcott were originally on the committee of the Blandford Forum meeting. The Rev William Bishop, Harry Edgell and Samuel Bailward looked after the interests of the landowners, whilst John Billingsley and Samuel Kelston were already on the committee of the Somersetshire Coal Canal. This fact was of particular value as the meeting had resolved that the new committee

> ... be requested to confer with the Conductors of the Navigations lately projected from the Somerset Collieries, on the propriety and expediency of forming a junction with them wherever the two navigations may happen to approach each other.[16]

John Billingsley had further commitments as a promoter of the Bristol & Western Canal between Bristol and Taunton and was also actively concerned with the Kennet & Avon Canal. He was an outstanding agricultural expert and was vice-chairman and one of the founders of the Bath & West Society. His local interest included turnpike trusts and the ownership of Oakhill Brewery.[17] The Earl of Ilchester was also concerned with other canals and later took the chair at some of the meetings of the abortive Ivelchester & Langport Navigation.

The first meeting of the newly appointed D & S committee was fixed for 25 April at the Bear Inn, Wincanton, presumably to give sufficient time to find out which engineer or surveyor might be available to survey the two proposed lines of the D & S. The Canal Mania was still raging, with a consequent demand for competent canal engineers, and the committee were fortunate to secure the services of Robert Whitworth, consulting engineer to the Thames & Severn Canal.

CHAPTER 2

The Route is Agreed, 1793-5

DURING the time that Whitworth was making the survey of
the alternative routes proposed for the D & S, a similar survey
was being undertaken by John Rennie for the route of the
Somersetshire Coal Canal. A promotion meeting for the SCC
had been held at the Old Down Inn on 4 February 1793, several
colliery owners being present including those from Camerton,
Dunkerton, Paulton, Radstock and Timsbury (the northern
collieries) and Holcombe and Kilmersdon (the southern collieries). A committee was appointed

> ... with power to employ and direct one or more able engineer
> or engineers to survey, plan and make estimates of the expence
> of completing such lines of canal and branches for the accom-
> modation of the Northern collieries, as they may conceive most
> practicable and advantageous. And at the same time, that such
> engineer or engineers be directed to survey the expence of
> making a branch from the proposed canal to Radstock; from
> Radstock to such place or places as may to the Committee
> appear of general utility to the Southern collieries . . .[1]

The SCC deposited plans to show that the Radstock branch
of that canal was not intended to go farther than Welton, still
leaving the collieries at Holcombe and Kilmersdon without
canal communication. It is possible that this may have been
due to some arrangement between the SCC and D & S committees, because a resolution was passed at a D & S meeting on
5 September:

> That as a great part of the tonnage expected on the proposed
> Canal must necessarily arise from the carriage of Coals, it

appears to this Committee, that a collateral branch from the coal pits on Mendip, to join this proposed Canal at or near Frome will be necessary. . . .[2]

The main purpose of the meeting of 5 September was to discuss Robert Whitworth's report of his survey. He estimated that it would cost £100,234 to complete the 37 miles of canal from Freshford, through Frome and Wincanton, to Stalbridge, and said that this section would be well supplied with water. From Stalbridge, two alternative routes to Poole had been surveyed, one via Sturminster Newton, Blandford and Wimborne (33 miles), the other via Lytchett Heath (31 miles). Either line would cost about £83,353 to cut and there would be no difficulty with water supplies, whichever one was chosen.

Whitworth also surveyed a proposed deviation from Stalbridge to Wareham by way of Kingstag bridge, Mappowder, Bingham's Melcombe and Dewlish, a distance of 30 miles. This would cost £91,080, but was not recommended as he doubted if there would be sufficient water available. The Wareham line also required heavy lockage and a pumping engine to pump water to the higher levels.

It had not been possible to calculate the tonnage likely to be provided on each of the three routes surveyed, though Whitworth was of the opinion that the line from Stalbridge to Poole via Wimborne would be the most suitable one 'provided the consents of the gentlemen, near whose seats the same must necessarily pass, can be obtained'. It seems that there was already some doubt about the support of the landowners on that section because Richard Messiter—the solicitor, and some of the committee were asked to call upon those concerned

> . . . to confer with them on the mode by which the Canal can be carried on with the least possible inconvenience to them, and to solicit their concurrence and support.

Similarly, the committee chairman, the Rev Samuel Farewell, and others, including John Billingsley, were asked to talk with the colliery owners and landowners who would be affected if the branch from Frome were cut. Chief of these landowners was Col T. S. Horner, the head of a distinguished county family, who lived at Mells Park and owned most of the land in the vicinity.

At the conclusion of his report, Whitworth said he was too busy to undertake any more surveys on behalf of the D & S but recommended his assistant, William Bennet. Bennet had previously worked on surveys for extensions of the Manchester, Bolton & Bury Canal from Bolton to Red Moss to join the Leeds & Liverpool, and from Bury to Sladen and towards Sowerby Bridge as an alternative to the Rochdale Canal. He also surveyed the proposed Haslingden Canal, authorised in 1794 from Bury to Accrington on the Leeds & Liverpool, but never built.[3] As Bennet was available, the D & S committee agreed to employ him as surveyor, a decision influenced by Whitworth's offer of further assistance when required.

Besides carrying out an intensive survey of the route of the D & S, Bennet was also engaged during 1794 in a survey for the proposed Ivelchester & Langport Navigation. It is hardly surprising that his survey for the D & S committee was not completed until June 1795. At long last, on 3 July 1795, a meeting was held at the Town Hall, Wincanton, 'then and there to take the said Survey into Consideration'.[4] The advantages of the canal were set out in the advertisement for this meeting:

By means of the said proposed Canal a direct Communication will be formed with Bath, London, the Northern, Eastern and Southern parts of the kingdom with the Southern Collieries of Mendip, and with the Somerset Coal Canals, which lead to the Paulton, Radstock and other collieries on the Northern side of Mendip.

The Somersetshire Coal Canal Act[5] had received the Royal Assent on 17 April 1794, long before the D & S committee and landowners met to approve Bennet's survey. The SCC was planned to join the Kennet & Avon Canal at Limpley Stoke and Bennet suggested that the D & S might also link with the K & A at that point. The D & S committee thought otherwise and decided that a slight alteration to the junction point 'would be more beneficial to the public'. Bennet was ordered to make a new survey for this section of the route and to report his findings to the next meeting of the committee on 23 July.

The expenses of obtaining an Act of Parliament and in carrying the canal into execution were estimated at £200,000. The solicitor, Richard Messiter, was instructed to receive subscriptions in shares of not less than £100 each, a deposit of £3 per cent to be paid for each share. One-third of the total subscription was to be reserved for the landowners.

Samuel Kelston, a committee man who owned land at Beckington, was chairman at the committee meeting held on 23 July at the George Inn, Frome.[6] Bennet had surveyed a revised line for the D & S from Rode Common via Beckington to Widbrook, where it was now intended to join the K & A, and found this to be more suitable than the route suggested at the previous meeting. His suggestion was adopted. Samuel Kelston's landed interests were safeguarded by a clause which was later inserted into the 1796 D & S Act. This clause stipulated that no portion of the canal could be cut through his property until the D & S had purchased all land he might wish to sell.

The entire route of the canal was finally approved at a meeting held at the Crown Inn, Blandford Forum on 13 August 1795. John Lester was in the chair when the following resolution was passed:

> Resolved—That the said proposed Canal be carried from the port of Poole by the Towns of Blandford, Sturminster-Newton and Stalbridge in the county of Dorset, and the towns of Wincanton and Frome in the county of Somerset, through Beckington and Road in the said county, to join the Kennet and Avon Canal at or near a place called Widbrook, near the junction of the Wilts and Berks Canal with the said Kennet and Avon, with a branch from the said intended Canal from or near a place called Pinnel's Lake to Wareham, and another branch from the same, from or near Ham-Gate into Hamworthy. . . .[7]

The branch from Frome along the Nettlebridge valley was also approved. It would be provided with a valuable source of trade from the collieries at Stratton-on-the-Fosse, Holcombe, Edford, Vobster and Coleford and from the flourishing iron-works business owned by James Fussell. Fussell was a share-holder in the D & S and later designed a 'balance lock' for use on the canal[8] (the term 'balance lock' is the eighteenth-century equivalent of the modern 'boat lift').

Fussell's ironworks were at Mells, where could be found

> ... two iron forges which at this period are carrying on a trade little inferior, in point of extension, to those in the northern part of this Kingdom. All the Western counties are supplied at these manufactories with every iron implement of husbandry, and their connexions extend to the European and American continents.[9]

The statutory notice of intention to apply for a Parliamentary Act 'for making and maintaining' the Dorset & Somerset Canal was published in the *Bath Journal*, *Salisbury Journal* and *London Gazette* for three consecutive issues.[10] Powers were also to be sought for 'Rail or Carriage Ways or Stone Roads' to enable the Mendip collieries to be connected with the branch line from Frome to Nettlebridge. Plans of the canal were deposited with the clerk of the peace for Somerset on 30 November 1795 and with the clerk for Dorset.

Evidently some attempt was made to meet the wishes of the landowners affected, as a plan for a new cut at Fiddleford Water, Sturminster Newton was prepared by William Cluett, land surveyor. This would have taken the canal across the road from Sturminster Newton on a two-arched aqueduct. It showed that the D & S was intended to be built as a narrow canal, having a depth of 9ft in that particular section and a width of 15ft at the water level.[11] (See page 52.)

Some landowners were still dissatisfied and called a meeting at the Crown Inn, Blandford Forum, for Wednesday, 25 November 'to consider of the advantages and disadvantages' that the D & S might bring.[12] It appears that the organisers of the meeting did not gain the support they desired, as the following week they advertised:

SEVERAL gentlemen, proprietors of lands in the line of the intended CANAL from BRISTOL to POOLE, having met in consequence of an advertisement in the Salisbury and Sherborne papers, at the Crown Inn, at Blandford, and not finding either the Solicitor of the Bill, or any information or document submitted to them from the Chairman of the Wincanton Committee, to shew the advantages likely to accrue to the public from making the said proposed Canal; and having from mature consideration great reason to doubt the public utility of the same, have determined to request a further Meeting of the Gentlemen concerned therein, to be held on Tuesday the 8th day of December next, at the Crown Inn, at Blandford, at twelve o'clock at noon, when it is hoped that every information which the Solicitor, Surveyor, and other persons concerned can possibly give, will be laid before them.[13]

A list of fifteen names was appended, including that of Thomas H. Bastard who had been on the committee elected at Blandford Forum in January 1793. The Bastards were a famous Blandford family of builder architects and two of them had helped to rebuild the town after a disastrous fire had swept through the place in 1731.

It is not known if Richard Messiter, William Bennet or any of the D & S committee did respond to this latest advertisement and provide the information required. It is probable that it was ignored, because no account of it appeared in the local newspapers. There was no doubt that the opposition caused considerable concern, as the subscribers met at the Bear Inn, Wincanton, on 1 February 1796, 'to consider and determine on the measures to be adopted'[14] to obtain a Parliamentary Act. It was decided to go ahead but, to avoid the difficulties arising from the opposition, a drastic decision was taken. This was to abandon the proposed route south of Gains Cross near Sturminster Newton, on the Blandford road, together with the branches from Ham to Hamworthy and Lytchett Minster to Wareham.

New plans were drawn, in accordance with the foregoing decision, before the House of Lords Select Committee met on 22 March.[15] The list of landowners, which had been presented

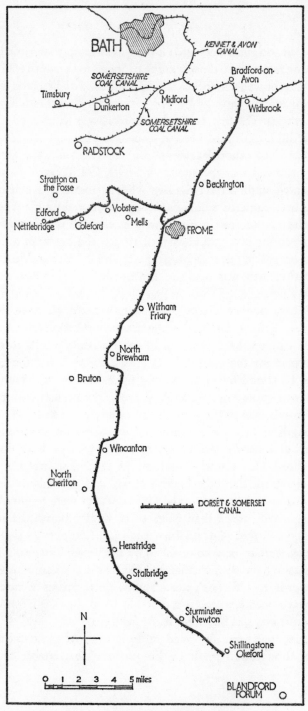

Map 1. The canal as authorised, 1796

with the original deposited plans, was simply amended by deleting reference to those owning property to the south of Gains Cross. It showed whether each owner assented or dissented to the canal being cut through his property and included two significant entries. The first noted that Lord Rivers 'consented if the Canal did not proceed beyond some point betwixt Sturminster & Blandford otherwise witholding his consent'. The second entry showed that the squire of Mells, Col Thomas Horner, 'dissented until certain Clauses were introduced which have since been done & which have been approved by his Agent'. Despite his interest in canals as a committee member of the neighbouring scc, Col Horner obviously did not wish to have the D & S passing near to his property and it is noticeable that a wide diversion was made to the north of Vobster to avoid Mells Park.

William Bennet, George Messiter, Richard Messiter, John Bowles, Robert Gray, George Pearson Cook and Charles Thick formed the deputation to the House of Lords to state their case for the D & S Bill. Bennet estimated that the canal could be completed at a cost of £146,018, compared with the £200,000 quoted by him in July 1795. The reduction in price was mainly due to the shortening of the main line to 48 miles in length, which had avoided the necessity of a 1½ mile long tunnel at Lytchett Matravers and another ½ mile long one at Blandford. One tunnel would still be needed at Brewham, to pass under the Earl of Ilchester's coach road, and this would be 1,009yd long. The major engineering works were required for lockage, with more than 368ft to be overcome on the main line and a further 264ft on the branch line. The various changes in level were to be accomplished by the use of 'caissons'. This appears to have been an afterthought by the D & S committee as the words 'by Caissons', which follow the estimates of lockage, etc, have been written by a different hand. (A full account of the estimates will be found in Appendix 2.)

Bennet had been appointed engineer to the scc in November 1795, though still retaining his position as engineer to the

D & S.[16] Whilst at work on the SCC he must have met Robert Weldon, one of the sub-engineers, who was also an inventor. Weldon had patented a 'Hydrostatick or Caisson-Lock' in 1792,[17] describing it as 'A Machine or Contrivance for Conveying Vessels or Other Weights from an Upper to a Lower, or Lower to an Upper Level, on Canals'. Following a successful demonstration of this lift on the Shropshire Canal in 1794,[18] the SCC and K & A made an agreement to share the cost of erecting another such lift on the SCC. Weldon was employed as sub-engineer for this purpose and doubtless convinced Bennet that the lockage problems on the D & S could also be overcome by the use of boat lifts.

The House of Lords Select Committee was told that subscriptions to shares amounted to £79,200. The major subscribers were Edward Barnard (£1,000); Sir Charles Warwick Bampfylde Bt (£2,000); John Billingsley (£3,500); William Dean (£1,000); Rev Samuel Farewell (£4,000); James Fussell (£1,000); John Gibbs (£1,000); John Lambert (£4,000); Richard Perkins (£3,500); John Ring (£1,000); Samuel Robard (£2,000) and Job White (£3,500). Like John Billingsley, Richard Perkins was also on the committee of the SCC.

Amongst the minor shareholders were members of the Messiter family. Uriah, one of the brothers of Richard Messiter held £300 in shares. Another brother, John, who was Rector of Marsh Caundle, Dorset, held £500 and a sister, Letitia, £100.

In view of the influential support for the D & S Bill, it is not surprising that there was no delay; and

> An Act for making a Navigable Canal from or near *Gain's Cross*, in the Parish of *Shillingston Okeford*, in the County of *Dorset*, to communicate with the *Kennet* and *Avon* Canal, at or near *Widbrook*, in the County of *Wilts*, and also a certain Navigable Branch from the intended Canal

received the Royal Assent on 24 March 1796,[19] two days after the select committee had met.

CHAPTER 3

Construction Begins, 1796-8

Now that the Act had been passed, 'The Company of the Proprietors of the Dorset and Somerset Canal Navigation' could elect from amongst their number a committee of twenty-one persons, each one having to hold at least three shares. The Act stipulated that the first general assembly should be held at Wincanton on 20 June 'for putting this Act in Execution'.

The decision to terminate the southern end of the canal at Gain's Cross, owing to the opposition of the landowners, had defeated the original purpose of the D & S, which was to provide an inland communication between Poole and Bristol. The expected coal traffic from the Mendip collieries still made the canal a viable proposition, and the Act laid down that the branch line from Nettlebridge to Frome had to be completed before work commenced on any portion of the main line. Not only had the canal to be navigable for boats between those two points, but also 'the several Rail or Carriage Ways, or Stone Roads, to communicate therewith' were to be made passable for carts and wagons.

In so far as the actual cutting of the canal was concerned, not more than 30yd width of land was to be taken for this purpose. The 30yd was considered to be adequate for the course of the canal, towing path and any ditches, drains and fencing that might be required. However, where wharves, reservoirs or passing places were to be made, up to 100yd in width of land might be taken.

The D & S proprietors had powers to take water from any

Page 33 (*above*) Bridge over the canal at Edford that carried the pack-horse track from Stratton Common; (*below*) 'Hucky Duck'—Coleford aqueduct, northern face

Page 34 (*above*) Uncompleted 'balance lock' at Barrow hill, with remains of centre partition of lock chamber in foreground; (*below*) Murtry aqueduct, western face

source within 2,000yd of the canal, including that raised by pumping engines from the collieries within this radius. Similarly, any mines were not to be worked to the prejudice of the navigation, though the mineral rights of land acquired by the D & S remained with the previous owner.

The following rates of tonnage were authorised:

For all Coal, Culm, and Coke, which shall be carried on the said Branch of Canal leading from *Nettlebridge* to *Frome*, as far as to the Point of Junction with the said intended Canal, at or near the Field in the Occupation of *Samuel Humphrys*, or which shall be carried to any Wharf in the Town of *Frome*, One Shilling and Sixpence *per* Ton, subject nevertheless to the Proviso herein-after mentioned:

For all Coal, Culm, and Coke, which shall be carried on the said intended Canal, except the aforesaid Branch from *Nettlebridge* to *Frome*, Two-pence Halfpenny *per* Ton *per* Mile:

For all Dung, Peat, Peat Ashes, and all other Ashes, intended to be used for Manure, all Chalk, Marle, Clay, and Sand, Lime, and all other Articles intended to be used for Manure, and all Materials for the repairing of Roads which shall be carried on the said intended Canal, or Branch, One Penny Halfpenny *per* Ton *per* Mile:

For all Iron, Iron Stone, Pig Iron, Iron Ore, Bar Iron, Coper Ore, Lead Ore, Calamine, Lime (except what shall be intended for Manure), Lime Stone, and other Stones or Minerals, Bricks and Tiles, which shall be carried on the said intended Canal or Branch, Two-pence Halfpenny *per* Ton *per* Mile:

For all Cinders, Charcoal, Corn, and other Grain, Pulse, Flour, Malt, Meal, Timber, and Wood, which shall be carried on the said intended Canal or Branch, Three-pence *per* Ton *per* Mile:

For all Cattle, Sheep, Swine, and other Beasts, which shall be carried on the said intended Canal or Branch, Four-pence *per* Ton *per* Mile:

For all other Goods, Wares, Merchandise, and Commodities whatsoever, which shall be carried on the said intended Canal or Branch, Four-pence *per* Ton *per* Mile:

For all Coal, Culm, Coke, and other Goods, which shall be carried on such Rail or Carriage Ways, or any or either of them, Two-pence *per* Ton *per* Mile:

C

And so in proportion for any Quantity less than a Ton, and for any Distance less than a Mile.[1]

The D & S was also empowered to take a toll for every horse or head of cattle passing over the rail or carriage ways, except on occasions when the animals were simply being moved from one field to another. All tolls were payable only once a day, irrespective of the number of movements of the vessel or animal concerned.

Col Horner received a special concessionary rate of toll, the Act reciting that not more than two pence per ton per mile was to be charged on any coal, culm or coke 'which may be raised or made on or under any of the Lands belonging to Thomas Horner Esquire' and carried on the branch line.[2] All landowners were entitled to use pleasure boats on the canal without payment, providing that these craft did not exceed 12ft in length and 5ft in breadth and did not make use of the locks.

Although the D & S Act gave powers to make a junction with the K & A, this was to be on a level without any form of lockage leading into or out of the canal. No trace of any agreement between the two companies can be found in the K & A minute books, but the attitude of the K & A committee was made clear in a previous proposal for a junction with an intended canal from Newbury to Basingstoke. The K & A could see no defect in that proposal, but could not recommend its inclusion in the K & A Bill then proceeding through Parliament 'as it had been their uniform practice to decline all interference with other concerns'.[3]

The first general assembly of the D & S proprietors was held at the Town Hall, Wincanton. Besides electing the committee, the meeting appointed Richard Messiter and his brother Uriah to the post of clerks and treasurers to the company. It was ordered that a seal be made. Tracings of the few surviving impressions show that a canal scene was depicted, with a boat proceeding in either direction, each being towed by the mast. Behind this canal scene the land rose and the hills were crowned

ANNO TRICESIMO SEXTO

Georgii III. Regis.

CAP. XLVII.

An Act for making a Navigable Canal from or near *Gain's Croſs*, in the Pariſh of *Shillingſton Okeford*, in the County of *Dorſet*, to communicate with the *Kennet* and *Avon* Canal, at or near *Widbrook*, in the County of *Wilts*, and alſo a certain Navigable Branch from the intended Canal.

[24th *March* 1796.]

WHEREAS the making and maintaining a Navigable Preamble.
Canal for Boats, Barges, and other Veſſels, from or near a Place called *Gain's Croſs*, within the Pariſh of *Shillingſton Okeford*, in the County of *Dorſet*, to join and communicate with the *Kennet* and *Avon* Canal, at or near *Widbrook*, in the Pariſh of *Bradford*, in the County of *Wilts*; and alſo the Navigable Branch herein-after deſcribed, from the ſaid intended Canal, will open an eaſy and convenient Communication with many conſiderable manufacturing Towns and Places in the Country through which the ſame are intended to paſs, and alſo with the extenſive Collieries near *Mendip*, in the County of *Somerſet*; and will render the Conveyance of Goods, Wares, and Merchandize, Coal, Stone, Slate, Flags, Lime, Limeſtone, Timber, and other Things, leſs expenſive than at preſent, and will be of great publick Utility: But the ſame

6 Z 2 cannot

Title-page of the Act of 1796 for the Dorset & Somerset Canal

FIG 1. The first page of the Dorset & Somerset Canal Act, 1796

by a slender tower. In the foreground were two recumbent figures, and the whole seal was bordered by the legend 'DORSET AND SOMERSET CANAL COMPANY 1796'.

Even before the general assembly had been held, plans were afoot for construction work to commence, and it was announced in mid-June that the committee would meet at the Talbot Inn, Mells, on 27 June 1796:

> for the purpose of agreeing with any person or persons who may be desirous of contracting for the Cutting, Embanking, Puddling and Compleating in a proper and effectual manner, a certain Part of the Branch from the intended Canal leading from the Mendip Collieries to Frome, extended from Coat, in the parish of Stratton-on-the-Fosse, in the said county of Somerset, to Upper Vobster in the parish of Mells aforesaid; being in length about four miles and for building the several Culverts, Road and Occupation Bridges, in the said Line of Canal, and making an Aqueduct across Grove-Valley at Coleford.
>
> The above will be let in one or more lots agreeably to the offers that may be made. . . .[4]

Plans for this first length were to be had from John Bowles, the sub-engineer. It was essential to have capital to finance the construction work and the general assembly of 20 June approved that a call of £7 should be made on each share, in addition to the £3 deposit already paid.

The committee had no success in its attempts to obtain a tender for the 4 mile length of canal from Stratton Common to Upper Vobster and readvertised for contracts in smaller lots the following month. The Bath, Bristol, Birmingham, Gloucester and Sherborne newspapers carried the new advertisement:

> Lot II. From a certain point in a field, called Tomlin's, in the occupation of John Padfield, to the East Side of the Road near the Meeting House at Coleford.
> Lot III. From the end of Lot II to Luckington-lane.
> Lot IV. From Luckington-lane to Upper Vobster.[5]

An aqueduct was to be made in Lot II and a tunnel in Lot III. The D & S was authorised to continue from Stratton Common as far as the Bath–Shepton Mallet turnpike road at Nettle-bridge, and to acquire the tollhouse at that point. The Shepton Mallet Turnpike Trust minute books contain no indication of any negotiations with the D & S committee and it remains a minor mystery why the canal was never cut to the west of Stratton Common.

The second advertisement for tenders was more successful and it was reported in September:[6]

> We hear that the Dorset and Somerset Canal advances very rapidly in its progress, and that the public will soon begin to experience the benefits that must arise from this undertaking; part of it near the collieries is already completed, and a barge was launched there on Monday.

As there are no records of any commercial traffic on the canal, the barge referred to above must have been a vessel used by the contractors.

The progress on the D & S was not to the satisfaction of all the shareholders and John Frankland, one of the committee men, wrote to the clerks to ask if the deposits already made on shares could now be refunded. He received this reply:[7]

> Dear Sir,
>   I beg leave to acquaint you that the Company of Proprietors of the Dorset and Somerset Canal do not consider themselves as liable to refund any of the Deposits which they have received from persons becoming Subscribers to that Concern and after-wards declining their Subscriptions. At the same time I have no Doubt but they would consent to let such persons, or their representatives have the number of shares in the Scheme— which they originally subscribed for, on paying up the different Calls which have been since made. I am happy in saying that the Work is very rapidly proceeding and in a very satisfactory manner.

<table>
<tr><td></td><td>Dear Sir</td></tr>
<tr><td>Wincanton</td><td>Your obed. & humble St.</td></tr>
<tr><td>2d Sept 1797</td><td>Uriah Messiter</td></tr>
</table>

Further calls had been made on shares at the general meeting held in Wincanton Town Hall on 5 December 1796, when a call of £5 per share was made[8] and at a special general meeting at the George Inn, Frome, on 24 April 1797, when £10 was requested upon each share.[9] Other work had been let out to contract, namely 'a lot of cutting from Elliott's Lane in the parish of Elm . . . to a certain point near Bradford's Bridge in the parish of Frome Selwood . . . about 7 furlongs'.[10] This contract included the masonry work and bridges also, and the building of a small aqueduct over the river near Murtry Mill. Plans were available from William Bennet.

The special general meeting at Frome had been called to receive a report from Bennet about the proposed aqueduct near Frome. Evidently construction of the Murtry aqueduct began soon afterwards, as is evidenced by a mason's mark inside a small tunnel underneath the southern end of the aqueduct.

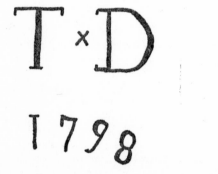

FIG 2. Mason's mark on the wall of a tunnel beneath Murtry aqueduct

Another length of the canal was put up for tender in May 1797:[11]

> To be let, at the Talbot Inn, Mells, on Monday May 15th. Lot of cutting on this Canal from a certain pound in an Orchard occupied by Mr. Nash in the Parish of Great Elm to Dye-house Lane in the Parish of Frome Selwood being 1 mile 5 furlongs, or thereabout with the masonry thereon, consisting of several Road and Occupation Bridges, Culverts, etc. The whole to be

cut, built and completed in a proper and effectual manner, agreeably to the Plans, Sections and Specifications thereof, which may be seen at the House of Mr. Bennet the Engineer at Stoney Lane, Nr Frome, or the George Inn, Frome.

The Person contracting to find security for the performance of his contract, and all Persons contracting are required to take Notice, that no Proposal will be received after 12. o'clock.

So far, the section of the canal requiring the use of boat lifts had not been put to tender. The D & S committee were no doubt awaiting the results of Weldon's lift on the scc. It was still being built in 1797 and, though the brick-lined lock chamber was completed by June, the tunnel leading to the lower level was not watertight. The 'caisson lock' consisted of a water-tight wooden box (the caisson) large enough to hold a 20 or 30 ton narrow boat, which rose and fell by means of racks and pinions within a masonry chamber full of water in which the wooden box was totally immersed. The caisson closely fitted a movable gate at both the top and bottom levels of the lock chamber, thus enabling boats to enter and leave through sliding doorways in the caisson itself, even though the lock chamber remained full of water. The dimensions of the lock chamber were: height from foundations to top—88ft; width—20ft in the middle narrowing to 11½ft at each end; length 88ft.[12]

Progress on the scc was faster elsewhere. In June 1797 it was anticipated that 11 miles of that canal would be completed in about eight months time, whilst 6 miles had not yet been put up for tender. The caisson could be raised and lowered within the lock chamber by November, but it was not yet ready for use. The additional work and finance required for Weldon's lift began to place a strain on the scc finances, a strain which was increased when the long awaited trial took place on Friday, 12 February 1798. A part of the apparatus gave way, breaking off the guide wheels, and leaving the caisson sus-pended at an angle in the lock chamber. A contemporary report of this accident[13] mentioned that it should be repaired within six weeks or two months, though the optimism was not to be matched by events. A successful demonstration was held on 4 June but the scc committee wisely decided that more trials should be held before they could recommend its use for that canal. The foresight was justified, because the lift soon became unworkable through repeated failures, and Weldon spent most of the winter repairing his defective invention.

The D & S committee continued its policy of awaiting results from Weldon's boat lift by deferring any work on the canal locks near Mells. Elsewhere on the D & S branch line, building continued. Some shareholders were reluctant to pay calls on their shares, even though interest at the rate of 5 per cent pa was allowed on all former calls from 4 December 1797.[14] It was agreed that all those in arrears with calls should be sued for payment.

One reason for this reluctance to make payment may have been the decline in the woollen industry. Frome, with a population of about 10,000 people and Shepton Mallet, with a further 6,000, were both dependent upon this trade. In Frome alone, one-third of the town were employed in the manufacture of woollen cloth, the annual output being over 150,000yd. There was strong opposition to the introduction of power-looms and rioting had taken place at nearby Bradford-on-Avon in 1791. A similar situation occurred at Trowbridge, when displaced workers set fire to a mill where the hated new machinery had been installed. The Rev Samuel Farewell, the first chairman of the D & S management committee, was intimately caught up with this distress in his duties as incumbent of Wincanton, and took an active part in helping to relieve those affected, until his death on 30 January 1797.[15]

Power-looms needed coal, and coal was plentiful along the route of the branch line to Nettlebridge. John Billingsley, as a committee man of both the D & S and scc, had an obvious interest in the modernisation of the woollen industry and wrote:

Machinery *must* and *will* be universally introduced, otherwise the districts, where *it is not used*, must be sacrificed to those where *it is*. Would the legislature interfere to suspend its operations, or limit its progress? This would be incompatible with its wisdom and justice. To allow only its *partial establishment* would be oppressive; to admit of *none*, would be ruinous; because such machinery, with its appendant branches of manufacture, and a *few individuals* allotted to each, is not only susceptible of, but it is presumed will shortly be, in a state of migration. In Yorkshire, where it has received a degree of perfection, and an extent of establishment, beyond that of any other part of the kingdom, I have been informed, from indisputable authority, that before the present war, the great demand for the produce of the manufactures left few, in comparison, to resort to agriculture for support.[16]

CHAPTER 4

The Balance Lock, 1799-1802

UNLIKE the woollen industry, the Mendip iron industry was still flourishing and James Fussell, one of the ironmasters, patented a 'Balance Lock for Raising or Lowering Boats, &c.' on 24 December 1798.[1] It was of a simple design and, as Fussell was on the committee of the D & S, was soon to be adopted for use on the canal instead of Weldon's lift.

Weldon's invention had been under repair throughout the winter of 1798-9 and was eventually ready for demonstration on Saturday, 27 April 1799. The Prince of Wales and his suite were present at the trial and the Prince expressed 'his entire approbation' of the lift.[2] Weldon's success was shortlived because water caused the walls of the lock chamber to bulge in May, thus rendering it useless until such time as it was again repaired. The SCC sought advice from its own engineering staff and from Benjamin Outram, engineer of the Peak Forest Canal. In commenting on the various reports submitted, William Bennet, engineer to both the SCC and D & S, drew attention to Fussell's invention in April 1800:[3]

> The next mode of getting from the upper to the lowel level proposed, is by the Geometrical or Balance Lock proposed by Mr. Fussell, and also by Messrs. Whitmore and Norton, which if completely effected, offers to be one of the most expeditious modes of lockage hitherto proposed, with all the advantages of the Caisson principle in respect to saving water, which seems to be a desirable object; and should the scheme answer the desired effect, will be as simple in its application, as any other plan that has been proposed. . . .

44

But as you have now an opportunity of having a trial on a similar plan to the Geometrical lock, by Mr. Fussell, on the Dorset and Somerset Canal, in the course of two Months from this time, without any risk or expence whatever, will it not be advisable to wait until the event of such trial, you will then be able to form a better judgement of it.

Fussell's lift itself was divided into two parallel pits by a partition wall of the same width as each of the chambers. The upper and lower levels of the canal were likewise divided into two channels. Barges were floated into large watertight boxes open at the top, made of wood or iron. These boxes exactly fitting the channels of the canal and the lock chambers. There were hatches at each end of the receptacles, and stop-gates to control the water at either level. Then the receptacles were simultaneously raised and lowered, like a pair of balance scales, by means of an arrangement of wheels and chains, depending ultimately on a beam placed across the partition wall which divided the lock into two.[4] (A technical description of the lift will be found in Appendix 3.)

The trial of the lift, anticipated to take place in June, was delayed until September 1800. In the meantime there had been some changes on the D & S committee. At the general meeting on 2 December 1799 there were three vacancies to fill and William Salkeld, Richard Pew and Rev William Ireland were appointed.[5] The meeting also received a report from John Paget, chairman of the committee of management, on the state and progress of the works. There had been some difficulties in cutting Lot III from Coleford to Luckington lane and John Rennie had been called in to examine this section:

At the request of Messrs. R. & U. Messiter I have examined in company with Mr. Bennet the proposed alteration of the Dorset and Somerset Canal near Coleford and have made Estimates both of the Expence of Tunnelling under the Hill by Goodeaves Colliery and of going round it in open Cutting; the Expence will be pretty nearly agreeable to sections furnished me by Mr. Bennet etc.

The Length of Tunnelling requisite in this Situation is about

320 yards—the Stratas are very irregular and will not hold water
—of course it must be lined, a Tunnel made in this way cannot
cost less than £10 p. yard, which makes the whole amount to
£3200.

The Length in going round by Mr. Bennet's Section appears
to be about 1547 yards, and the Expence by my Estimate about
£2650 exclusive of the Expence of an Act of Parliament which
I expect will bring it nearly to the amount of the Tunnel. Had
the ground through which the Tunnel must pass (if made) been
perfectly sound i.e. had none of it been underworked, I should
have had no hesitation in giving a preference to the Tunnel on
account of the great saving in length being nearly three-fourths
of a mile, but as there is great reason to believe that the ground
is very unsound and of course liable to sink I should hesitate
much in Recommending a Tunnel here, the ground adjacent
round is also underworked and perhaps is liable to give way as
under the Tunnel, yet whatever failures happen in the open
cutting can easily be repaired. But were a failure to happen in the
Tunnel I scarcely know how it could be repaired, I have therefore no hesitation in giving my decided Opinion in favour of
the circuitous Line.[6]

Rennie's opinion was not accepted, despite the dire conse-
quences he foretold should the tunnel be made. Perhaps the
D & S committee did not want to go to the trouble and expense
of obtaining another Act of Parliament. The tunnel, never
completed, now lies buried beneath a rubbish dump, though
part of the cuttings on either side of Goodeaves hill can still be
seen. Stories have been told of blocks of dressed stone lying
about in the cuttings before the rubbish dump obliterated all.[7]

The first trial of Fussell's lift took place at Barrow Hill near
Mells on Saturday, 6 September 1800. The experiment was
made on a fall of 20ft and laden boats transferred up and down
between the two levels 'in much less time than is usually employed in passing',[8] though the invention was capable of a
lift of more than 40ft.

Elated by success, the D & S committee gave notice that a
public exhibition of the lift would be given on Monday, 13
October and said it was found 'to be a cheaper and more
expeditious mode of transferring Boats than any other that has

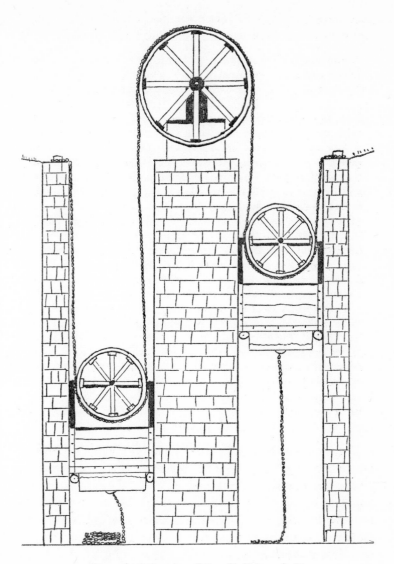

FIG 3. An impression of Fussell's 'balance lock'

been hitherto adopted'.[9] The correspondent of the local press was equally enthusiastic when the exhibition took place:

A trial was made on Monday last according to the notice on the Dorset and Somerset Canal of a Balance Lock, the invention of Mr. Fussell, at Mells, near which place it is erected and to whom it is but justice to announce that it answered the design perfectly to the satisfaction of a great number of spectators: among them were many men of science, impartial and unprejudiced, who after its repeated operations and those without the least difficulty of mischance, and inspecting minutely every part of the machine, were unanimous in declaring it to be the simplest and best of all methods yet discovered for conveying boats from the different levels and for public utility.—The expence of it exceeds but little that of the common lock, over which it has these advantages viz. it elevates a boat of ten tons burthen and sinks another of equal weight by the same operation twenty feet perpendicular in half the time that one boat passes the common lock and this with a trifling loss of water; a circumstance so valuable that it must render its use general. —The proprietors of the undertaking must be highly gratified to be in the hands of a gentleman whose first effort of the kind has been so fortunate and who has insured its success at the outset in a great measure by his superintendance and unwearied attention on the executive part of his machine and by giving every necessary instruction in its progress to the different workmen concerned; the neglect of which is a circumstance much to be lamented by a neighbouring engineer (Mr. Weldon) on account of the failure of his Caisson-Lock at Combhay.[10]

The scc committee had spent £4,582 on Weldon's lift up to December 1799[11] and decided that the expense of a further £1,000 on repairs was not justified. This decision ended all hopes of Weldon's invention. In its report on the trial of Fussell's lift, the *Bath Chronicle* suggested that another of the same type would replace the now useless 'caisson lock' on the scc. This was not to be, for the scc committee decided to use an inclined plane to link the upper and lower levels of the Dunkerton arm of its canal. Later, in 1805, the inclined plane was replaced by the conventional form of lockage.[12]

The D & S committee was very satisfied with Fussell's lift and, following a general meeting at Wincanton Town Hall on 1 December 1800, decided to erect five similar lifts on the canal between Mells and Frome.[13] Tenders were to be delivered to the committee at the Talbot Inn, Mells, on Friday, 13 February 1801, at 12 noon. Friday the thirteenth was, perhaps an inauspicious day to choose, if anyone was superstitious; however, no harm resulted and contracts were exchanged, so allowing work to begin on the locks.

A call of £5 per share made at the general meeting held at the George Inn, Frome, on 15 August 1801, meant that each share was now fully paid-up.[14] Earlier calls had been as follows:

Call	When made	£
Deposit	3 July 1795	3 [15]
1st	20 June 1796	7 [16]
2nd	5 December 1796	5 [17]
3rd	24 April 1797	10 [18]
4th	4 December 1797	10 [19]
5th	19 June 1798	10 [20]
6th	3 December 1798	10 [21]
7th	13 September 1799	10 [22]
8th	10 April 1800	10 [23]
9th	1 December 1800	10 [24]
10th	10 April 1801	10 [25]
		—
		95

In February 1802 the financial position had worsened and the D & S committee asked all persons having a claim against the concern to submit the same to the clerks, Messrs Messiter of Wincanton, to be examined and reported upon at the next meeting.[26] In the meantime William Underhill, engineer of the Dudley Canal, had been commissioned to survey the works already completed and report on the amount of money required to finish the branch line to Welch Mill, Frome. He was also requested to discover 'the quantity of Coals now raised and which may be hereafter raised from the different collieries on the line of the Canal'.[27]

But why had this financial crisis arisen? When the first pro-

motion meeting was held at Wincanton in 1793 the scheme was
so popular that people came from all parts of the county, and
some even travelled from Manchester and Birmingham, to seek
shares in the undertaking. Soon after, the French War broke
out and altered the prospects of the canal, capital being ab-
sorbed in loans to the Government by those who would otherwise have subscribed to the D & S.

> The alarm of invasion was felt, taxes were levied, the price of
> labour advanced, and the spirit of improvement which had
> begun to rise in the nation was checked and suspended by the
> various active preparations for an arduous warfare.[28]

Even the D & S committee was occupied in more pressing
tasks. Richard Messiter, for example, organised and was captain
of a troop of the East Somerset Yeomanry which he fed and
clothed at his own expense.[29]

Although the 1796 D & S Act gave powers to raise £150,000,
the amount actually subscribed was between £60,000 and
£70,000, and of that only £58,000 was ever paid-up. Much of
this latter sum was spent in obtaining the Act, in purchasing
land and in making compensation for trespass.[30]

Mr Underhill's report was read to a general assembly of the
proprietors at the George Inn, Frome, on 23 March. It was
stated that £18,000 more would be needed to complete the
branch line.[31] The meeting unanimously resolved that the
works should be finished and the navigation opened to Frome.
The clerks to the company were instructed to prepare a draft
Bill, so that application might be made to Parliament for powers
to raise more money. This was to be achieved by the creation
of new shares, at a price to be agreed upon at a later meeting.

Action was to be taken against those proprietors who were
in arrears with the payment of calls. A list of such names was
read to the assembly and the clerk was ordered to write and
warn them that their shares would be forfeited if all arrears
due were not immediately paid. As an inducement to prompt
payment, a short account of the canal's prospects appeared in
the newspaper advertisements reporting this meeting:

Page 51 (*above*) Canal bed, to the east of Murtry aqueduct; (*below*) The 'Roman wall' at Frome—canal embanking

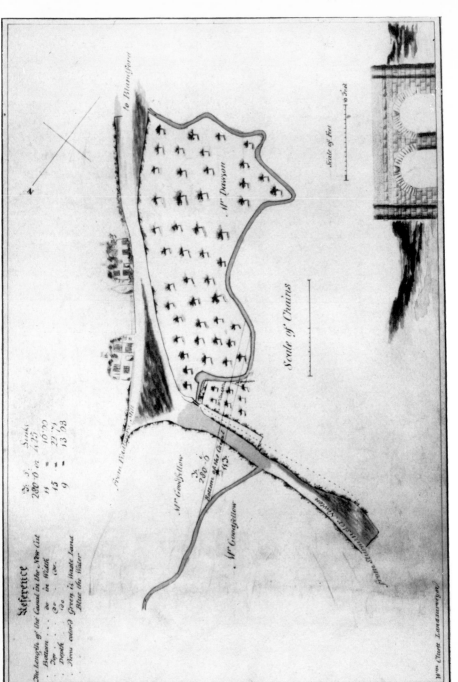

Reference

The Length of the Canal in the New Cut

Bottom . . . . do in Width
Top . . . . do . do.
Depth . . . . do . do.

Brown colored Green is Waste Land
Blue the Water

to Blandford

Mr Dawson

Mr Goodfellow

Mr Goodfellow

From Fiddleford Mill

Bottom of the Canal

Scale of Feet

Scale of Chains

Wm Clark Landsurveyor

Page 53. Plan of proposed 'new cut' at Fiddleford Water, Sturminster Newton

The Proprietors will be gratified to hear that there never was a period when this undertaking appeared of so much importance as at the present moment. The tonnage upon Coal and Lime, but more especially upon LIME, to supply the continually increasing wants of the lands contiguous to the Kennet and Avon and Wilts and Berks Canals (independant of every other species of tonnage) affords prospect of a revenue which exceeds all calculation.[32]

The Kennet & Avon Canal had been completed between Bath and Foxhanger Farm, below Devizes on 1 May 1801. The Widcombe flight of locks, which would connect the K & A at Bath with the Avon Navigation, was still under construction and a temporary connection was made by means of a stone roadway. Similarly, a horse-drawn iron railway connected the canal at Foxhanger Farm with the town of Devizes during the time that the great flight of locks at Caen hill was being built.[33]

The Wilts & Berks Canal was navigable from Semington, the junction with the K & A, to Wootton Bassett and to Calne, the latter being served by a branch line. At the end of 1802 the W & B committee reported that 'the demand for Somersetshire Coal is now become very great' and that 'the Dorset and Somerset Canal, which will also communicate with this, we are informed is taken up with spirit, and will produce an additional supply of Lime, Stone, Coal, and other articles'.[34]

The Somersetshire Coal Canal had been opened between the coal pits at Timsbury and the junction with the K & A, at Limpley Stoke, in November 1801 and made possible a large saving in transport costs for coal. Even before it was fully completed, in May 1799, there had been a reduction from 10s (50p) to 2s (10p) per load on coal destined for Bath.[35]

In spite of the shortage of money, work continued on the D & S as normal whilst there was still some cash left to pay the contractors. The committee staged a third demonstration of Fussell's lift on 3 June 1802, again with complete success and praise from the press:

D

The principle on which it acts is so perfect that boats of *any burthen* may be conveyed by it with the greatest facility and one of its chief recommendations is the simplicity of its construction which can scarcely ever render it liable to repair.[36]

Soon afterwards, in September, the usual statutory notice was published to show that the D & S intended to make application in the next session of Parliament for a Bill to alter and amend the existing Act, and also 'for the purpose of raising a further sum of money beyond what has already been advanced'.[37]

CHAPTER 5

In Stagnation, 1803-25

IN 1803 the money ran out and work on the canal had to stop. A special assembly of the proprietors was held at the George Inn, Frome, on 30 March, 'for the purpose of taking into consideration the situation of the concern and determining powers to be applied for to Parliament, in order to the further prosecution of the said undertaking'.[1] This meeting was called by five of the committee—John Paget, Richard Perkins, Thomas Davis, Job White and James Fussell. It was agreed that the management committee should go ahead with the application for an Act, despite the upset of the times.

Britain had made peace with France in 1802 by the Treaty of Amiens, but within a year war had broken out again and there was a very real threat of invasion from across the Channel. Once more thoughts of the canal were dropped whilst attention was directed towards repelling any invasion by Napoleon. James Fussell made a patriotic gesture in August 1803:

> At this eventful and momentous crisis, when the heart of every Briton beats high with true loyalty and patriotism, we feel pleasure in recording the spirited offers made to the Government for the defence of the country. Mr. James Fussell, of the Mells Iron Factory, near Frome, has offered to prepare (gratis) 1,000 pikes, and afterwards to supply the Government with 2,000 weekly as long as they may be wanted.[2]

A few weeks earlier, on 20 June, the House of Lords Select Committee sat to hear the application for the second D & S Act. George Messiter appeared on behalf of the proprietors but had

55

not, apparently, been fully briefed as there were several in-
accuracies in his evidence. He stated that 11 miles of the branch
line had already been cut and that the company had only been
able to raise about £65,000 under the 1796 Act. (The correct
figures were nearly 8 miles and £56,479 respectively!) There
was a debt of £1,100 owing for construction work, but the
sum to be raised by the new Act, in addition to that allowed by
the former Act would be sufficient to meet all debts and to
complete the canal.[3]

The application was successful and on 4 July 1803,

> An Act for enabling the Company of Proprietors of the Dor-
> set and Somerset Canal Navigation to raise a further sum of
> Money towards completing the said Canal, and for altering and
> amending an Act passed in the Thirty-sixth Year of the Reign
> of his present Majesty, for making and maintaining the said
> Navigation

received the Royal Assent.[4] It authorised the raising of more
money by means of promissory notes at 5 per cent interest pa,
giving the lenders the option of becoming shareholders by the
conversion of these notes into shares. There were also powers
to allow the substitution of a railway, instead of canal, upon
any part of the line that might be thought expedient.

By the time that construction work ceased, the following had
been completed:

13 Arched Bridges, built with excellent materials.
 5 Swivel Bridges.
 5 Fixed Bridges.
 2 Draw Bridges.
11 Grooved Stop Gates.
 9 Double Stop Gates.
19 Trunks.
 6 Waste Weirs.
26 Culverts and Drains.
 2 Tunnels.
 1 Tunnel, at a place called Goodeaves (only 90 yards complete).
 1 Balance Dock, complete.
   Two others partly finished.[5]

The 'Balance Dock' was almost certainly a printer's error for Fussell's 'balance lock'. In addition to the works listed above, there was 'a noble and stupendous Aqueduct at Coleford'. An inscribed stone from this aqueduct was found in the rockery of a house called *The Chantry* at Little Elm, near Mells.[6] The house was built by James Fussell's eldest son, also named James, about 1825 and the stone bears the words:

AQUÆDUCT
ERE ANNO 1801

Immediately above the top of this inscription is a break in the stone, though the bottom of another line of writing can be seen, and the letters COLEFORD are indicated.

FIG 4. Inscribed plaque from Coleford aqueduct

The two tunnels which figure in the list are a complete mystery. No trace of any tunnel, other than the cuttings leading to Goodeaves hill, are visible and it may be that they were simply places where the canal passed under a road which had a wider bridge than usual. No trace, either, remains of the milestones which were to be erected at half-mile intervals.[7]

Fears of invasion persisted throughout the remainder of 1803 and the D & S committee resolved 'to suspend the works until more auspicious times arrived'.[8] The decision was influenced by the great difficulty in raising money, the attention of the public being diverted to the military preparations and alarms of the time. Some maintenance did, however, continue because Alexander Rogers was paid various sums of money for repairs to the canal.[9]

About $1\frac{3}{4}$ miles of the branch line remained uncut. There was a length of about 1 mile from Barrow hill to Elliotts and the remainder was between Whatcombe Farm and the junction with the main line at Frome. A Frome-Selwood parish map of 1813[10] shows the canal terminating in a dead end to the north-east of Whatcombe Farm, without any canal basin. This length was built partially on a hillside and has a long stretch of walled embanking known locally as 'the Roman wall'. The western-most end of the branch line was not completed either and the 1840 tithe map of Stratton-on-the-Fosse[11] reveals that a rect-angular basin was made where the canal terminated at Stratton Common. No work had been started at any point on the main line.

Now the construction work had ceased on the D & S, William Bennet was able to turn his attention wholly towards the SCC. He had plenty to occupy his time with the building of the Combe Hay flight of locks, twenty-two of these replacing the inclined plane which had been found unsatisfactory in use. Another flight of nineteen locks was intended to link the Radstock arm of the SCC with the main line at Midford.

Like the D & S, the SCC had to raise more money, but as that canal was already in use there was less difficulty in setting up a 'Lock Fund'. This was subscribed to equally by the K & A, W & B and SCC, each of whom contributed £15,000. Bennet grossly underestimated the costs, the work on the Combe Hay locks alone being over £7,300 more than anticipated.[12] The same fault affected the finances of the D & S for, some thirty years later, it was said 'by some injudicious management, the subscriptions were expended, before the work was near com-pletion'.[13] By 1808 Bennet was engaged in some work for the K & A, having left the service of the SCC soon after his estimates had been found to be incorrect. In 1812, he was described as an engineer and land surveyor of 32 St James's Parade, Bath,[14] and it must have been in this capacity that he was consulted by the Worcester & Birmingham Canal committee:

> A letter from Mr. Bennet, Engineer, Bath, respecting a Machine for raising and lowering Vessels instead of locks in reply to one written to him by Mr. Parker for Information on that subject.
>
> Resolved that Mr. Parker write again to Mr. Bennet thanking him for his letter & request he will have the Goodness to inform this Committee whether the Machine on the Dorset & Somerset Canal is now in use & the strength of the brickwork and any other particulars he may think worth communicating.[15]

Even the K & A were of the opinion that the D & S was suspended for but a short while and, perhaps even more surprising, thought that the section from Gains Cross to Poole would eventually be cut. The writer of the earliest-known guide book on the K & A, which was published in 1811, mentioned that when the D & S was continued from Sturminster to Poole the whole southern coast of Dorset would be opened up to the coal, corn and iron trade.[16] The optimism seemed general, as a history of Somerset published in 1813[17] included a map showing both the main and branch line of the D & S!

John Billingsley did not live to see the publication of this map. He died at his home, Ashwick Grove (now demolished), on 26 September 1811 and is buried close by in Ashwick churchyard, after a lifetime of service to his county of Somerset.

Richard Messiter, one of the clerks and treasurers, severed his connection with the canal for different reasons. 'Possessing an ardent mind, he was of too speculative a disposition, which led him into difficulties'.[18] He became bankrupt in 1819 and emigrated to America, being granted an allowance by his brothers Uriah and George. He died and was buried there in 1830.

The long years of the Napoleonic Wars came to an end in 1815 and peace was achieved after the Battle of Waterloo. Once again men were able to turn fully to their own affairs, though with the end of the war also came a slump. The depression in

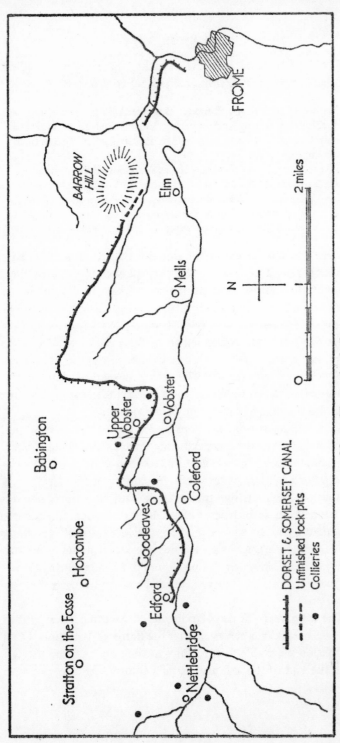

Map 2. The canal as built, 1803

the coal trade can best be illustrated by the following figures, which show traffic originating from the neighbouring SCC:

Year	Tons
1814–15*	81,751
1816	76,079
1817	74,115

* Year commencing 29 May

The colliery owners tried to recoup some of their losses by a reduction in wages, and the imposition of a 10 per cent cut at the end of February 1817 provoked a strike at Paulton. This quickly spread to involve the miners at Clandown, Clutton, High Littleton and Radstock and, owing to the gravity of the situation, the Riot Act was read and the military called in to restore order. The troops included a detachment of the North Somerset Yeomanry Cavalry, under the command of Col T. S. Horner of Mells Park. By Tuesday, 4 March, the strike was over and the miners all back at work, apart from five ringleaders who were arrested and later sentenced at Taunton Assizes to terms of imprisonment.

This local disturbance, coupled with the general depression in trade, had the effect of delaying any immediate revival of the D & S. A revival did eventually take place, but as an offshoot of one of the many schemes projected for railways, following experiments with steam power in the North of England.

In 1813 a young engineer, George Stephenson, was at work at Killingworth, near Newcastle-upon-Tyne, building his first steam locomotive. In the following years he turned out a succession of engines and Killingworth became the 'Mecca' for all railway promoters interested in steam power. A successful colliery railway system, the 8 mile long Hetton Colliery Railway, was opened on 18 November 1822 and included portions of the line worked by locomotives, others by stationary engines and some by inclined planes! A new dimension in travel became possible and the first public railway to use locomotives, the Stockton & Darlington Railway, was ceremoniously opened on 17 September 1825.[19]

OLD-DOWN INN, March 4, 1817.

AT a Special Meeting of the Magistrates acting in and near the Hundreds of Chew and Chewton, in the County of Somerset, and of the several Gentlemen, Clergy, and Owners and Occupiers of Lands, resident in such Hundreds and their Vicinity, whose hands are hereunto subscribed, holden at the above Time and Place;

Col. T. STRANGWAYS HORNER, in the Chair:

Resolved,

THAT the thanks of this Meeting be given to Sir JOHN COX HIPPISLEY, Bart. M. P. for his communication of a letter written by him, to the Right Honorable Viscount Sidmouth, his Majesty's Secretary of State for the Home Department, detailing the late tumultuous and riotous conduct and proceedings of many of the Workmen employed in several of the Coal Mines at Paulton and that neighborhood, (in the sentiments and statements of which letter they most cordially concur), and for those prompt, decisive, and effective measures suggested and adopted by him, which have so happily and speedily restored tranquillity to this part of the County.

Resolved,

THAT the thanks of this Meeting be given to THOMAS SAMUEL JOLIFFE, Esq. for the ready and able assistance which he afforded by his accidental though most opportune appearance at Radstoke at a moment when his influence was most beneficially exerted.

Resolved,

THAT the thanks of this Meeting be given to the COMMANDING OFFICER of his Majesty's Military Forces at BRISTOL for the promptitude with which he forwarded a Detachment of the 23d Reg. of Lancers, and to the Officers, Non-Commissioned Officers and Privates forming that Detachment; and also to COL. STRANGWAYS HORNER, and the Officers, Non-Commissioned Officers, and Privates of the North Somerset Yeomanry Cavalry, for the great alacrity, zeal, and patience which they respectively evinced, and for the valuable services which they afforded on this occasion: And also to CAPT. TUSON, and the Officers, Non Commissioned Officers, and Privates of the Wells Troop of Yeomanry Cavalry for holding themselves in readiness to render their assistance.

Resolved,

THAT this Meeting, notwithstanding they deeply feel, and most sincerely deplore, the distresses and difficulties with which it hath pleased the Almighty " to visit his people," yet they cannot attribute the late disorderly conduct of their Neighbours wholly to this afflicting circumstance, inasmuch as they consider that these violent measures have been, in a great degree, resorted to from the perusal and effect of various blasphemous and revolutionary publications, which, they lament to state, have been so long industriously, and almost gratuitously, circulated amongst them.

Resolved,

THAT this Meeting, duly and gratefully appreciating the many blessings they enjoy under their present happy form of Government, are determined to sustain the present period of trial and suffering with fortitude and resignation; and although they will be at all times ready and anxious to alleviate the real distresses of their less opulent neighbours, they will never cease to use their utmost powers and exertions in protecting and defending themselves, and their Rights and Properties, as well against the efforts of a tumultuous and misguided Multitude, as against the delusive, and more dangerous schemes and machinations of visionary and disaffected Speculators.

Resolved,

THAT the Chairman be requested to transmit these Resolutions to Lord Viscount Sidmouth; and also to the different persons whose services are considered to have been so highly valuable; and that the same be published in the Courier, Felix Farley's Journal and the Mirror Bristol Papers, in the Sherborne Mercury, and all the Bath Papers.

Resolved,

THAT the Thanks of this Meeting be given to the Chairman, for his able conduct in the Chair, and his great and polite attention and services in the business of the day.

T. STRANGWAYS HORNER,
CHAIRMAN.

Mells-Park, near Frome.

HENRY GOULD, ... *Wells*
FRANCIS DRAKE, ... *Wells*
THOMAS WILLIAMS, ... *Camley*
W. B. BARTER, ... *Timsbury*
WILLIAM COXETER JAMES .. *Timsbury*
J. S. PHILLOTT .... *Wookey*
JOHN FREDERICK DOVETON, *Marksbury*

Acting Magistrates for the County of Somerset.

Peter Gunning, D. D. *Farmborough*
Charles Knatchbull, *Babington-House*
G. Mogg. *Farrington-Gurney*
Jacob Mogg, *Ditto*
William Kelson, *Midsomer-Norton*
William Read, Clerk, *Ditto*
Richard Boodle, Clerk, *Radstock*
John Skinner, Clerk, *Camerton*
P. Edward Scobell, M. D. *Hallatrow*
Thomas B. Johnston, Clerk, *Clutton*
Rees Mogg, Clerk, *Cholwell*
John Brookes, Clerk, *Hinton-Blewett*
William Wright, Clerk, *East-Harptree*
Charles Wayland, Clerk, *Litton*
John Goldfinch, *Chewton-Priory*
Henry Hodges Mogg, Clerk, *Ston-Easton*
John Parish, Captain R. N. *Timsbury*
George Scobell, Captain R. N. *Hallatrow*
Farnham Flower, *Chilcompton*, Surgeon

William Rawlins, *Paulton*
James Crang, *Hallatrow*, Surgeon
James Flower, *Chilcompton*, Surgeon
Thomas Miles, *Ston-Easton*
James Eyre Salmon, *Holcombe*
Joseph Hill, *Paulton*
Richard Langford, *Hallatrow*
Joseph Hill, Jun. *Paulton*
R. B. Thornhill, *North Somerset Yeomanry*
James Rawlins, Clerk, *Paulton*
Thomas Hollwey, *Welton*
Robert Langford, *Timsbury*
Thomas Ames Hill, *Paulton*
John Saunders, *Paulton*
Thomas Powell Lansdown, *Paulton*
George Hill, *Paulton*
William Brodribb, *Clutton*
James Perrin, *Temple-Cloud*
James Dudden, *Temple-Cloud*

Richard Cox, *Hallatrow*
John Brodribb, *North-End*
James Harris, *Clutton*
Francis Bowcher Wright, *Hinton-Blewett*
John Raynes, *Compton-Martin*
George Pope, *East-Harptree*
William Lord, *Chewton Parsonage*
S. D. Witherell, *Lytton*
George Wright, *East-Harptree*
Charles Ozen, *Ditto*
Francis T. Doolan, *Hinton-Blewett*, Surgeon
James Isles Choppin, *Hallatrow*, Surgeon
John James, *Hallatrow*
Thomas James, *Hallatrow*
Thomas Flower, *Hallatrow*
William Williams, *High-Littleton*
Thomas Collier Dudden, *Hallatrow*
William Boulter, *Marksbury*
James Weaver, *Marksbury*

FIG 5. The aftermath of the Paulton strike, 1817

The news of the various experiments and successful operations had spread to the West of England and an advertisement on the subject appeared at the end of August 1825:[20]

TO THE LANDHOLDERS, AND OTHERS WHOM IT MAY CONCERN

In consequence of many Persons having expressed an opinion that a RAIL-ROAD would be highly beneficial between the Bristol Channel and Basingstoke, in Hampshire, which should traverse the Blue Lias Stone Quarries, and connect itself with the Collieries on Mendip, it has been proposed that a MEETING should be called on MONDAY, the 12th day of SEPTEMBER next, at *Wincanton*, to take into consideration the propriety of applying to Parliament, for leave to bring in a Bill to lay down a Rail-Road from the mouth of the River *Parrett*, near *Bridgwater*, to run along *Polden Hill* to *Street*, through *Butleigh* to *Keinton*, to *North Cadbury*, *Mapperton*, *Wincanton*, *Gillingham*, *Shaftesbury*, *Hindon*, *Wilton*, *Salisbury*, *Andover*, and *Overton* to *Basingstoke*; with a branch from or near *Gillingham*, to the north and east of *Wincanton*, to or near *Bruton*, to the Collieries on *Mendip*.

Several Gentlemen who have given this project their serious consideration will attend, and be prepared to explain, in detail, the advantages likely to result from the undertaking as well as to lay before the Meeting such other information and explanation as may be required; from plans and estimates already formed.

It is therefore hoped that a full attendance will be given by Gentlemen interested in the internal trade of the county of Somerset, since the projected Work can be executed for a sum comparatively trifling, when the great advantages that must result are considered.

The chair will be taken at twelve o'clock, at the Greyhound Inn, in Wincanton.

August 15th, 1825.

It was stated that the projected railway was sanctioned by some of 'the most respectable and opulent inhabitants of this county' and that several of the landholders had already expressed their desire to subscribe freely to the project.[21]

CHAPTER 6

The Western Railway, 1825

THE promotion meeting for the proposed railway from the Bristol Channel to Basingstoke was postponed two days until Wednesday, 14 September 1825. Owing to the number of people who wished to attend the venue, too, was changed to the Town Hall, Wincanton, and the chair was taken by William Dickinson MP.

The plan of the railway was described in great detail by Sir Thomas Buckler Lethbridge Bt, who had previously been concerned with the promotion of an English & Bristol Channels Ship Canal.[1] This canal was to run from Stolford, on the Parrett estuary, to Beer by way of Creech St Michael, Ilminster and Chard. An Act was passed on 6 July 1825[2] and authorised the raising of £175,000 capital, though it stipulated that no work was to commence on the canal until this capital was fully subscribed.

The estimated cost of the railway was also £175,000, allowing approximately £2,000 a mile for the 82 miles from the mouth of the Parrett to Basingstoke, and making some allowance for the 43 miles of branches. The engineer, Josiah Easton, had also been concerned with a scheme to link the English and Bristol Channels and in 1793 had surveyed the route for a canal from Axmouth, near Seaton, to Axminster, Chard, Ilminster, Creech St Michael, Bridgwater, Huntspill and Congresbury to serve the collieries at Backwell, near Nailsea.[3] Later, in 1795, he was in charge of construction work on the Ivelchester & Langport Navigation.[4]

64

Easton had devised a 'Patent Stone-Road' upon which steam locomotives could be worked, propelling 40 tons of coal at the rate of 6 mph. His invention had already been given a 'slight' trial and had worked successfully though, in the event of its failure, the railway could be used with the wagons drawn by horses.

The price of coal at Basingstoke would be reduced from 30s (£1.50) to 15s (75p) per ton, and this still allowed 5s (25p) per ton for carriage costs as the price at the pithead was 10s (50p) per ton. Basingstoke was badly served by transport. The Basingstoke Canal, which joined the river Wey, had opened in 1794[5] and was charging 6s 2d (31p) per ton for coal conveyed the 37 miles of its length, apart from the tolls on the Wey and Thames.[6]

Sir T. B. Lethbridge explained that, since he had come to the meeting, he had learnt that the proprietors of the D & S had a vested interest in that part of the line proposed between the Mendip collieries, Frome, Bradford-on-Avon and Poole, because they already had powers to construct either a canal or railway. Although this presented an obstacle to part of the plans, the difficulty might be only apparent 'as arrangements might be made to accommodate all the parties concerned'.

Mr W. D. Bayley, a holder of shares in the D & S agreed, and said that a meeting of the proprietors had been held the previous Monday, at which he was appointed to attend the present one and propose a junction between the two undertakings. He suggested that the D & S should be built westwards to Wincanton and join with the railway at that point. This proposal was recommended by others present. He continued:

> The shares of the Dorset and Somerset Canal scarcely bear nominal prices at this time, and are literally worth nothing, unless by public exertion. They have sold for less than £5 per share, although they originally cost £100. In fact the Company can do nothing without a new subscription.[7]

To overcome this difficulty, he suggested that new shares should be created, each of £25 in value, which would rank as

Dorſet and Somerſet Canal.

—————•●◌❘◂❮❙❱▸❘◌●•—————

No. 309.

—————•●◌❘◂❮❙❱▸❘◌●•—————

Purſuant to an Act of Parliament paſſed in the Thirty-ſixth Year of the Reign of King GEORGE the IIId. intituled,

> " An Act for making a Navigable Canal from or near Gains-Croſs, in the Pariſh of Shillingſton-
> " Okeford, in the County of Dorſet, to communicate with the Kennet and Avon Canal, at
> " or near Widbrook, in the County of Wilts, and alſo a certain Navigable Branch from the
> " intended Canal."

This Ticket Certifies that *James Martin of Stalbridge in the County of Dorset Gentleman* . . . . is a Subſcriber to this Undertaking, and entitled to a Share therein, numbered *309.*

In Teſtimony whereof the Common Seal of the Company is hereunto affixed this *twenty first* Day of *June* . . . . . . One Thouſand Seven Hundred and Ninety *six*

} CLERKS TO THE
SAID COMPANY.

Fig 6. A share ticket

equal value with the existing shares, mentioning that a similar consolidation of shares on the K & A in 1801 had proved to be very successful. He concluded with some words of encouragement:

> The present Railway will run into our line and participate in our advantages; we on the other hand, shall feed and support the Railway; we heartily wish it success, and will lend it our support.[8]

The meeting resolved that the proposed railway from Stretcholt (a hamlet on the Parrett estuary near the village of

Pawlett) to the Mendip collieries by means of a junction with
the D & S, together with branches from Wincanton to Shaftesbury, Salisbury, Basingstoke, Sturminster Newton, Blandford
and Poole would be 'a highly desirable object'. A committee
was appointed: Hon Mr Ponsonby, Sir T. B. Lethbridge, John
Cree, Rev Dr Colston, Rev Harry Farr Yeatman, T. S. Bailward, Hubert Day, W. D. Bayley, Rev Samuel Blackall, Uriah
Messiter, Hyde S. Whalley, Thomas Davis, Charles Bowles
and Benjamin Gray. They were asked to consider the best
method of carrying the proposed Western Railway into effect
and to report their findings to the next public meeting. Josiah
Easton, who had surveyed the line, was requested to attend
the committee meetings with his plans and estimates and
Richard Welsh, a solicitor from Somerton, was appointed to
act as secretary.

The names of the D & S proprietors who had met to brief Mr
Bayley on the attitude to be taken towards the WR were
revealed soon afterwards. An advertisement calling a public
meeting of shareholders of the 'DORSET AND SOMERSET CANAL
AND RAIL-ROAD COMPANY' at the Town Hall, Wincanton, on
Monday, 24 October, was signed by James Fussell, T. S. Bail-
ward, H. S. Michell, J. White, F. Woodforde, Uriah Messiter,
Thomas Davis, E. Dyne and W. Bell, as well as by W. D.
Bayley. Its purpose was that

> . . . of considering the propriety of forming a JUNCTION
> with the Line of the projected WESTERN RAILWAY COM-
> PANY, or of adopting such other measures, and coming to
> such resolutions, as may be deemed expedient for the general
> benefit of the Shareholders, and of the public. . . .[9]

Supporters of the landed and commercial interests were also
invited to attend. The D & S revival had at last begun.

It was not as successful as had been hoped. A contemporary
report mentions that 'a long and desultory conversation took
place on the affairs and prospects of the Canal'.[10] This was chiefly
centred on the proposal by the WR committee to purchase the
interests of the D & S for £20,000. Eventually it was decided

that the meeting was not able to accept the offer made, probably because the committee elected by the proprietors were, with one exception, also on the WR committee! They were T. S. Bailward, Rev H. F. Yeatman, Thomas Davis, W. D. Bayley, Charles Bowles and Mr Fussell. The chairman of the meeting was William Dickinson MP, who had taken the chair at the earlier WR promotion meeting.

It was resolved that the D & S canal be completed as quickly as possible, especially the branch from the Nettlebridge collieries to Frome. To achieve this purpose, new shares should be offered at £25 each, to rank as equal with the existing shares, but no work was to start until sufficient money had been raised to complete the branch line. The committee was requested to advertise that any outstanding debts should be made known to the clerks, Messrs Messiter, so that this matter could receive attention at the next meeting.

A subscription deed was produced and approved. This had evidently been drawn up in a hurry, presumably by the ten proprietors who had called the meeting, because the pamphlet omits pages 12 and 13 and bears neither date or any other indication of its source. Simply headed *The Dorset and Somerset Canal Navigation*, it set out in great detail the advantages to be gained from completing the works, either as a canal or railway, whichever the committee might think fit.

The traffic from the Collieries to Frome, and from thence to Bradford, would be very considerable. Independently of Coal and Coke being obtained for the manufactories at Frome, Lime-stone may be had in any quantity, and is much wanted in the courses of the Wilts and Berks, and Kennet and Avon canals; and from the report of Mr. Underhill, who some time since surveyed the country, Ironstone and good Fire-clay are found, in a great variety of strata, on the line. The extensive Iron-works at Mells and Nunney, which have justly acquired so high a reputation, would find a Canal or Rail-road invaluable to their purposes, both in receiving the raw materials and conveying their manufactured goods; so it must be with the Messrs. Sheppards, of Frome, who, with few exceptions, are the only persons that keep up the high character of the fine cloths in the county of Somerset. Besides these, a considerable encouragement would be given to the small potteries at Wanstrow and Crockerton, for whose wares, a great demand would be experienced on the line of the Canal, even so far as the metropolis. The various manufacturers, the builders, the numerous retail tradesmen of Frome, and the public in general, could not fail to participate in these advantages, which would prepare the way for renewed industry, and prosperity in the town. But if the benefits would be thus considerable in executing the works as far as Bradford, they would be greatly enhanced if the communication were opened into Dorsetshire. The two distinct parts of the undertaking would supply and assist each other. Coals, coke, iron, potters-clay, freestone, lime, timber, wool, oil, cyder, and the various manufactures and products of the line, would be articles of constant traffic, and greatly encreased in demand; new manufactures would be elicited, and a fresh stimulus given to the old ones.[11]

The pamphlet noted that it would probably cost £18,000 to complete the branch line, and a further £35,000 if the main line was to be cut between Frome and Bradford-on-Avon to link with the K & A. To extend the main line westwards from Frome to Gains Cross would require an additional £100,000. It suggested that the work be completed according to the funds raised, so that if only sufficient money was obtained to finish the branch line, that alone should be completed.

Whilst the D & S proprietors were discussing the future of their canal, the WR committee had met several times to consider the plans and estimates of the proposed railway. A public meeting was called for Monday, 31 October, at the Ansford Inn, near Castle Cary to receive the report of the committee and for 'the adoption of such other measures as shall be agreed upon' for the promotion of the WR.[12]

Once again, the chair at the Ansford Inn meeting was taken by William Dickinson MP. The solicitor, Richard Welsh, read the report which stated that the WR committee had not been able to bring about an arrangement with the D & S committee, and so thought it best to alter the course of the proposed rail-

E

way to avoid interefering with the line of the D & S. Sir T. B. Lethbridge regretted that a junction had not been effected with the canal and that the D & S had refused the offer of £20,000 for its vested rights. In consequence of this refusal the engineer, Josiah Easton, had proposed a revised route. This was for a railway from Stretcholt to Somerton, to a point between Yeovil and Sherborne, thence by way of Piddletrenthide to Beer and Poole. The original route from Wincanton to Basingstoke had now been abandoned, a course which was not unwise, since it had been stated that the charges by canal from Basingstoke to London would be greater than the sea freight from Poole to London. When asked about possible opposition from the promoters of the English & Bristol Channels Ship Canal, Sir T. B. Lethbridge said that he thought it unlikely that any such opposition would arise.

For the D & S, Mr T. S. Bailward said that 'though no union had yet been effected with the Dorset and Somerset Canal Company, he did not think the door yet shut'.[13] His optimism was greater than that of the others attending this meeting, as is reflected in the resolution passed:

> That a Rail-Road from Stretcholt to Wincanton, to cross the Dorset and Somerset Canal, if it should be completed, so as to feed and supply the same, and be fed and supplied therefrom, upon terms advantageous to both . . . would be of the greatest advantage to the places and districts through which it should pass.[14]

It was decided to apply for an Act in the next session of Parliament to enable the resolution to be put into effect. The capital of the WR was to be £150,000 in shares of £50 each. Subscriptions were immediately opened, £1 deposit to be paid on each share to the treasurers, Messiter & Co of Wincanton.

One dissident voice had been heard during these proceedings. The Hon Capt William Waldegrave RN had asked for more details about the scheme, his attention having been drawn to the matter when he had discovered some strangers taking measurements and making surveys of land owned by his family. On making further enquiries he had learnt about the proposed railway. Sir T. B. Lethbridge undertook to give him the details requested.

The country landowners must have been more than a little confused when an advertisement for yet another proposed railway appeared in the press at the beginning of November. This stated that a meeting would be held at the Old Down Inn on Wednesday, 9 November 1825, to consider applying to Parliament for leave to bring in a Bill during the next session 'for laying down a RAILWAY from the collieries at Radstock and Neighbourhood to Hamworthy, near Poole Harbour'.[15] The advertisement had been submitted 'By order of several principal Landowners and Coal Proprietors' and was signed by Richard Welsh of Somerton, the secretary to the WR!

CHAPTER 7

The Radstock, Shaftesbury & Poole Railway, 1825-6

THE mystery about the proposed railway from the Radstock collieries to Poole was soon solved. On 9 November the prospectus of the Radstock, Shaftesbury & Poole Railway was read to those assembled at the Old Down Inn. The inn stood at the junction of the Bath to Wells and Bristol to Shepton Mallet roads and was a popular meeting place, the Somersetshire Coal Canal promotion meeting having been held at this same spot at the end of 1792. The colliery proprietors were present at the RS & PR meeting too, and one of their number, the Hon Capt William Waldegrave RN, whose family owned several of the Radstock collieries, took the chair.

The prospectus of the RS & PR stated 'The object of the Company is to establish an expeditious and cheap inland communication between the cities of Bristol and Bath and the harbour of Poole'.[1] The Somersetshire Coal Canal already provided a route between Radstock and Bath and Bristol, though it suffered from the disadvantage that the first 7 miles was by way of a horse-drawn tramway, making it necessary to transfer all goods into canal boats at Midford basin for onward transmission. It was explained that the RS & PR was being promoted in place of the WR with the blessing of Sir T. B. Lethbridge and other promoters of the earlier scheme.

The estimated expense of the new railway was £250,000 and it was proposed to raise capital of this amount by the issue of

2,500 shares, each of £100 in value. The motive power on the railway would be by the use of steam locomotives, enabling goods to be carried at not less than 6 mph by day or night and 'there was every reason to believe' that it might also be possible to carry passengers at speeds of 8 mph.

Thomas Davis, one of the D & S committee-men, spoke to say that 'should the intended Rail-Road interfere with the Dorset and Somersetshire Canal, it would be vigorously opposed by several Shareholders in that Company'.[2] Mr Bowles, another committee member, thought differently and said,

> that with respect to the Dorset and Somerset Canal, that was a measure which may or may not be completed, but in all events it ought not to interfere with a measure so feasible and so beneficial as the present. Though a subscriber, he would very gladly yield all advantages which might arise from it rather than it should be an impediment to this Rail-road. . . .[3]

Others felt even more strongly about the D & S. A Mr Spencer of Wells considered that a coalition with the canal company would be totally impossible and hoped that the RS & PR would have nothing to do with 'that cursed concern' as it would ruin the new undertaking altogether.

The meeting resolved:

> That a Railroad from or near the Collieries at Radstock and the neighbourhood, to Hamworthy, within Poole Harbour, to pass by or near the Towns of Frome, Warminster, Hindon, Shaftesbury, Blandford and Dorchester, would be of the greatest advantage to the places and districts through or near which it shall pass, and be productive of essential benefit to the public at large; as, by means of the Railroad and Canals already made between Radstock and the river Avon, at Bath, an expeditious and cheap inland communication would be made between Bath and Bristol and Poole Harbour.[4]

A committee was elected: Hon W. J. Ponsonby, Sir Thomas Buckler Lethbridge Bt, MP, Thomas Savage, Edmund Broderip jun, William Coxeter James, Hon Capt William Waldegrave RN, John Frederick Pinney, John Davis, Hyde S. Whalley, Capt Scobell RN and Capt Parish RN. Josiah and George

Easton were appointed engineers to the RS & PR, having previously occupied a similar position with the short-lived WR. Similarly, Richard Welsh retained his post of secretary to the new concern. New treasurers, Stuckey & Co, bankers of Langport, were appointed in place of Messiter & Co, no doubt because of the link between the latter company and the D & S.

It was decided that an Act of Parliament should be obtained in the next session, if possible. Subscriptions were immediately opened, £1 deposit to be made on each share. The editorial comment of the *Sherborne Mercury* was guarded: 'The line also appeared to meet with the general approbation . . . there is reason to believe little opposition is to be anticipated'.[5]

A further meeting to promote the RS & PR was held at the Grosvenor Arms Inn, Shaftesbury, on Friday, 11 November, with the Mayor, William Swyer as chairman. The resolution referring to the advantages of the railway was also passed at this meeting and new names were added to the committee. The new members were Lord Arundell & Wardour, William Swyer, Charles Bowles, John Cree, Rev Harry Farr Yeatman, Phillip Matthews Chitty, William Storey, John Hussey, Thomas Nash, John Clarke, Edward Spencer and Mr Rutter. Another resolution was approved, this limiting shares to a maximum holding of twenty-five for any one person.

Little time was wasted before the statutory notice of intention to apply for an Act of Parliament for the RS & PR was published, the details appearing in print only twelve days after the first gathering at the Old Down Inn.[6] Further support for the venture came from South Dorset when a meeting held at the Red Lion Inn, Wareham on 26 November, with John Calcraft MP as chairman, also gave approval to the proposed railway.

Mr W. D. Bayley, a member of the D & S committee, complained that though Uriah Messiter (on behalf of the D & S) and Hyde S. Whalley (on behalf of the RS & PR) had agreed to the sale of the canal interest for £20,000 'it was openly declared by some of the friends of the new measure that they did not declare the contract binding on them'.[7] He then said that the cost of completing the D & S as a railway from the Mendip collieries to Sturminster Newton, with a branch from Frome to Bradford-on-Avon would be £64,000 for a single-track line compared with the £300,000 revised estimate of the RS & PR. In an attempt to squash the opposition to the sale of the canal, he also remarked that 'The Dorset and Somerset Canal was in possession of corporate rights and of considerable land bought and paid for'.[8]

Another attempt to heal the breach between the two factions may have been influenced by Charles Bowles who, though a shareholder in the D & S, had been elected to the committee of the RS & PR by popular acclaim in the hope that he could act as mediator between the two parties. On 1 December, at the Crown Inn, Sturminster Newton, the following resolution was passed:

> That the apparent differences between the Proprietors of the Dorset and Somerset Canal and the Projectors of the Radstock, Shaftesbury and Poole Railroad, be submitted and, if possible, adjusted by the Committees of the two Parties.[9]

Mr Bayley had proposed that the canal should be completed to Sturminster Newton or Gains Cross and that the RS & PR should unite with the D & S at or near Vobster and run to Wincanton, Mere, Hindon, Shaftesbury and Salisbury.

General Michel and his neighbour, Mr J. Frampton, objected to the railway as it would cut through 9 miles of their property. General Michel stated that there was no need whatsoever for a railway in the southern part of Dorset, mentioning that best Newcastle coals could already be obtained at Weymouth for 11d (5p) per bushel and little extra elsewhere.

Owing to this opposition, and to the difficulties in completing the survey, it was agreed to defer the application for an Act of Parliament for the time being. The railroad project was still approved and it was resolved that the capital should be raised from £250,000 to £300,000, in view of the revised estimate and to allow interest at 5 per cent pa to be paid to the subscribers. On completion of the line it was anticipated that the tonnage would be sufficient to pay nearly 14 per cent pa in dividends.

The peacemaking moves between the two committees were successfully accomplished and by the end of the year agreement had been reached.

We notice with great satisfaction that the Dorset and Somerset Company appear to be adopting prompt measures for the prosecution of their work. The rival interests which have for the past few weeks attracted the attention of the west, are understood to be reconciled on a basis highly advantageous to the public, as well as to the supporters of the respective undertakings. The coals from both the northern and southern collieries are now to be brought into Dorset and Somerset by the Parliamentary line, and the new Radstoke Company are to branch off from the neighbourhood of Wincanton to Mere, Hindon, Salisbury and Shaston. The Dorset and Somerset line being the first part of the work to be executed, the Subscribers to that Company are proceeding to exercise the powers of their Act of Parliament, so far as they can be made available, and by that means prepare the way for the Radstoke Company, who will not be able to procure their Act until the Session after the next. . . .[10]

Once again things began to look more promising for the D & S and a special assembly of the proprietors was called for Thursday, 19 January 1826, to be held at the George Inn, Frome.[11] Its purpose was 'to choose 21 persons (proprietors of 3 or more shares) to be a Committee'. A sub-committee was to be appointed to examine and audit the accounts of the treasurer, clerks, engineer and other officers and servants of the company, prior to the meeting. The assembly was also to discuss the proposal of creating new shares of £25 each.

The special assembly met as planned, Mr T. S. Bailward of Horsington being chairman of the meeting. He explained that it was part of the business of the evening to solicit the consent of the old shareholders to the plan proposed for reviving the undertaking by the creation of new shares, and also to report upon the recent investigation into the company's accounts.

Messrs Tredgold & Bennet had previously estimated that a railway could be laid on the canal line from the Nettlebridge collieries to Frome for about £16,000, with another £24,000 if the extension to Wincanton were to be made. The total claims against the D & S did not exceed £6,000, but there was difficulty in reconciling those sent in with the amounts recorded in the company's books. Some, indeed, exceeded the book figures by a considerable amount, even when allowance for unpaid interest was made, and it seems that greed was the reason for the discrepancy between the debts recorded and those claimed.

It was recommended that the debts owing be taken in new shares, the sub-committee who investigated the accounts being of the opinion that 'it is impossible, in justice to new subscribers, to pay any part of the debts out of monies to be raised by the Shares'.[12] Mr Uriah Messiter said that, as treasurer to the D & S, he proposed to yield to the wish of the sub-committee and not only take the money owing to him in the form of new shares, but also to forgo the interest in the debt. He hoped that his example would be followed by others.

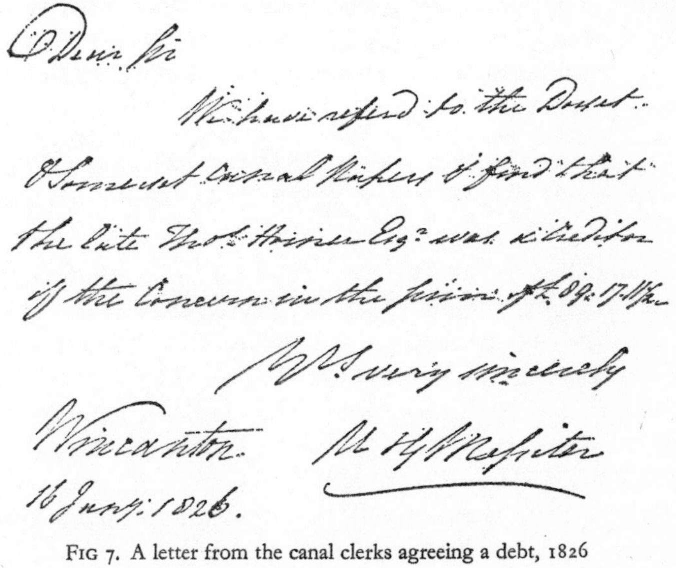

FIG 7. A letter from the canal clerks agreeing a debt, 1826

Whether the work should proceed or not, depended greatly upon the present Meeting; and, considering the great benefits which would result to the town and neighbourhood, he thought it not too much to expect that all, who could, would be ready to encourage and support a work which might at last fail, if they did not assist it. . . . He trusted the work might be completed, in the end, to Shillingstone; but it was wise to proceed from step to step, as resources could be supplied, and strength acquired.[13]

A 'desultory conversation' then took place about the claims upon the canal company, in which the irascible Mr Spencer of Wells took part. Mr Spencer had previously made known his feelings about the D & S during the course of RS & PR promotion meeting. James Fussell and Uriah Mesiter both said that they wished to remove every possible obstacle to the prosecution of the works and would therefore take their debts in shares, estimating these at £100 each, and thus effectively reducing the debt to 5s (25p) in the £.

A further objection came from Mr Shepherd and the Rev T. Shepherd, who considered that no business should be transacted until plans, surveys and specifications were laid before the meeting. The chairman, T. S. Bailward, thought that this was unreasonable at this stage and the meeting then unanimously resolved

. . . that it is expedient to revive the Dorset and Somerset Canal and Rail-Road by the creation of new Shares, at a reduced price of £25 each.[14]

A committee was elected, consisting of T. S. Bailward, Sir G. Bampfylde Bt, Thomas Davis, W. D. Bayley, Edward Dyne, J. S. Ward, Jos Brownjohn, Rev Walter Erle, Charles Bowles, James Fussell, Job White, Rev F. Woodforde, Rev John Messiter, Rev A. A. Askew, Richard Pew MD, John Francis, W. L. White, H. S. Michell, Rev H. Martin, Jas Fussell jun and Edward Hannam. Five of these members, Thomas Davis, W. D. Bayley, James Fussell, H. S. Michell and James Ward formed the subcommittee of management.

Several new shares had already been taken up by the landed gentry and other influential people in the county and it was also agreed that a further committee be formed, so that the interests of both the old and new shareholders could be represented on the D & S. Uriah and George Messiter were appointed as clerks and treasurers and Messrs Tredgold and Easton as surveyors and engineers.

In February 1826 the D & S clerks advertised:

All persons desirous of becoming SHAREHOLDERS in the projected RAILWAY, from the Mendip Collieries to FROME, WINCANTON and STURMINSTER are requested to send their names and the number of shares required to Messrs Messiter. . . .[15]

A footnote indicated that 'upwards of £10,000 has already been subscribed'. There was little, if any, response to this advertisement, for the year 1825 had seen an unprecedented failure of small country banks, particularly in the West of England, whilst a depression in the silk industry led to great distress for the weavers of Taunton, Sherborne, Shepton Mallet and Bruton. These were all towns near to the line of the proposed railway.

Although the *Sherborne Mercury* had given fulsome coverage to the special assembly of the D & S on 19 January, the true state of affairs was revealed by another west country newspaper which said 'there were not so many persons present as were expected'.[16] At that meeting Mr W. D. Bayley, in introducing the proposed plans, had said

. . . he knew the present period was unpropitious to enterprize; but he did not hesitate to say, that the plan was unrivalled in point of advantages, and would, at some day or other, be duly executed. . . .[17]

His words were soon proved to be true, for the desired capital was not subscribed. In consequence the scheme foundered through lack of support; and with the collapse of the D & S scheme also went the hopes of the RS & PR.

Epilogue

WHEN it was seen that the proposed D & S railway and the RS & PR project had both failed, the land gradually reverted to its original owners or their heirs and successors. Some sections still had water in them as late as 1840. The unpublished autobiography of Richard White of Mells refers to a journey he made to Bristol in the company of his uncle. They were delayed on the return trip, and his mother was so worried that she sent someone to make sure they had not met with an accident in the canal which ran through Holwell Farm.[1]

At the turn of this century an aged inhabitant testified that, in his youth, barges were navigated along the canal from Edford as far as the Greyhound Inn at Coleford.[2] Local legends often have a grain of truth in them, though the truth of this testimony may never be revealed.

In the late 1840s negotiations opened for the purchase of land required for the Frome to Radstock branch of the Wilts, Somerset & Weymouth Railway. Authorised in 1845, the line was not opened until 14 November 1854. The deeds include a conveyance dated 5 March 1850 from the Rev J. S. H. Horner to the WS & WR for almost 2 miles of land, including 'all that piece of land through which it was formerly intended a canal should pass'. The agreement to purchase, dated 31 January 1848, made provision for the railway company 'to be at liberty to deposit spoil in the old Canal so as to fill up the same or any part thereof without money payment'.[3] In some places this was done, making it impossible to trace the course of the D & S completely throughout this length.

Another scheme, the Nettlebridge Valley Railway, would also have affected the D & S. The deposited plans[4] show that it was intended to diverge from the Frome–Radstock branch of the WS & WR near Babington and thence run through Upper Vobster, Coleford, Edford and Edford Common to Nettlebridge. An Act of Parliament was obtained in 1874 but the scheme was abandoned in 1878.[5] Rail communication had earlier been made with two of the collieries, Mackintosh and Newbury, by means of a short private railway, connecting with the branch line near Mells Road station, and this was probably constructed about 1857.[6] The line was partly built on the bed of the canal, but some of the track was lifted in the autumn of 1969.

The remains of the canal are described in Appendix 1. There is little else to be found because armed conflict, neglect and the changing fashions of each age have all taken their toll. Bomb damage at Wincanton during the last war destroyed all records of the canal company and information now has to be gleaned from the pages of local newspapers. Occasionally a tablet on the wall of a parish church will record the connection of a worthy townsman with the canal or, at the very least, give details of his age and date of death. By such means is local history uncovered and with it the story of a project described as 'one of the best conceived undertakings ever designed for the counties of Dorset and Somerset'.[7]

Notes

NOTES TO CHAPTER 1 (*pages* 15-22)

1. J. Latimer, *Annals of Bristol in the Eighteenth Century*, 1893.
2. *Felix Farley's Bristol Journal*, 2 February 1793.
3. Ibid, 21 September 1793.
4. *Bath Chronicle*, 17 January 1793.
5. I am indebted to the county archivist, Somerset Record Office for this information.
6. Ibid. The pedigree of the Messiter family is to be found in *Burke's Landed Gentry*, 1914.
7. *Bath Chronicle*, 17 January 1793.
8. *Felix Farley's Bristol Journal*, 16 February 1793.
9. Ibid.
10. *Sherborne Mercury*, 4 February 1793.
11. Ibid.
12. Ibid, 18 February 1793.
13. 35 Geo III, c 105.
14. *Sherborne Mercury*, 11 February 1793.
15. *Felix Farley's Bristol Journal*, 6 April 1793.
16. Ibid.
17. For further details of John Billingsley, see Robin Atthill, *Old Mendip*, 1964, pp 45-54.

NOTES TO CHAPTER 2 (*pages* 23-31)

1. *Bath Chronicle*, 7 February 1793
2. *Felix Farley's Bristol Journal*, 21 September 1793.
3. I am grateful to Charles Hadfield for this information.
4. *Felix Farley's Bristol Journal*, 6 June 1795.
5. 34 Geo III, c 86.
6. *Bath Chronicle*, 30 July 1795.
7. *Felix Farley's Bristol Journal*, 29 August 1795.
8. For an account of James Fussell's life, see Robin Atthill, *Old Mendip*, 1964, pp 71-2.
9. J. Collinson, *History of Somerset*, 1791, Vol 2, p 461.
10. *Bath Journal*, 14, 21 and 28 September 1795; *Salisbury Journal*, 14, 21 and 28 September 1795 and *London Gazette*, 15, 19 and 22 September 1795.

11. Dorset Record Office, plan PL2.
12. *Sherborne Mercury*, 23 November 1795.
13. Ibid, 30 November 1795.
14. Ibid, 25 January 1796.
15. House of Lords Record Office Committee Book, H.L., 22 March 1796.
16. Somersetshire Coal Canal Minute Book, 3 November 1795.
17. No 1892 of 30 June 1792.
18. *Sherborne Mercury*, 13 October 1794.
19. 36 Geo III, c 47.

NOTES TO CHAPTER 3 (*pages 32–43*)

1. 36 Geo III, c 47, s XCIV.
2. Ibid, s XCV.
3. Kennet & Avon Canal Minute Book, 26 August 1793.
4. *Bath Chronicle*, 16 June 1796.
5. *Aris's Birmingham Gazette*, 4 July 1796.
6. *Sherborne Mercury*, 12 September 1796.
7. Dorset Record Office, accession 9455.
8. *Sherborne Mercury*, 2 January 1797.
9. Ibid, 8 May 1797.
10. Ibid, 27 March 1797.
11. *Aris's Birmingham Gazette*, 8 May 1797.
12. John Billingsley, *General View of the Agriculture of the County of Somerset*, 1798, 2nd ed, Appendix, p 317.
13. *Bath Chronicle*, 15 February 1798.
14. *Sherborne Mercury*, 25 December 1797.
15. George Sweetman, *The History of Wincanton*, 1903, p 56.
16. *General View of the Agriculture of the County of Somerset*, op cit, p 161.

NOTES TO CHAPTER 4 (*pages 44–54*)

1. Patent No 2284.
2. *Bath Journal*, 22 April 1799.
3. William Bennet's report to the Somersetshire Coal Canal committee, 2 April 1800.
4. I am grateful to Robin Atthill for this description.
5. *Sherborne Mercury*, 9 December 1799.
6. Rennie's MS report on the Dorset & Somerset Canal, 1799 (Institution of Civil Engineers).
7. Robin Atthill, *Old Mendip*, 1964, p 170.
8. *Gloucester Journal*, 15 September 1800.
9. *Bath Chronicle*, 2 October 1800.
10. Ibid, 16 October 1800.
11. Somersetshire Coal Canal Report, 7 December 1799.
12. For a full account of the 'caisson lock' and of the Somersetshire Coal Canal, see my *The Somersetshire Coal Canal and Railways*, 1970.
13. *Aris's Birmingham Gazette*, 26 January 1801.
14. *Bath Chronicle*, 27 August 1801.
15. *Felix Farley's Bristol Journal*, 11 July 1795.

16. *Sherborne Mercury*, 4 July 1796.
17. Ibid, 2 January 1797.
18. Ibid, 8 May 1797.
19. Ibid, 25 December 1797.
20. Ibid, 2 July 1798.
21. *Bath Chronicle*, 27 December 1798.
22. *Sherborne Mercury*, 23 September 1799.
23. *Bath Chronicle*, 17 April 1800.
24. Ibid, 11 December 1800.
25. *Bath Herald*, 18 April 1801.
26. *Bath Chronicle*, 11 February 1802.
27. Ibid.
28. *Sherborne Mercury*, 19 September 1825.
29. George Sweetman, *The History of Wincanton*, 1903, p. 216.
30. *Sherborne Mercury*, 19 September 1825.
31. *The Dorset and Somerset Canal Navigation*, n.d. (1825 ?) (Dorset Record Office & BTHR).
32. *Bath Chronicle*, 5 April 1802.
33. For a full account of this canal, see my *The Kennet & Avon Canal*, 1968.
34. For the history of the Wilts & Berks Canal, see Charles Hadfield, *The Canals of South and South East England*, 1969, pp 276–94.
35. *Gloucester Journal*, 13 May 1799.
36. *Bath Chronicle*, 10 June 1802.
37. Ibid, 9 September 1802.

NOTES TO CHAPTER 5 (*pages 55–63*)

1. *Bath Chronicle*, 17 March 1803.
2. *Bristol Journal*, 6 August 1803.
3. House of Lords Record Office Committee Book, H.L., 20 June 1803.
4. 43 Geo III, c 108.
5. *The Dorset and Somerset Canal Navigation*, op cit.
6. Robin Atthill, *Old Mendip*, 1964, p 170.
7. Rees' *Cyclopaedia*, article 'Canals', 1805.
8. *The Dorset and Somerset Canal Navigation*, op cit.
9. *Sherborne Mercury*, 30 January 1826.
10. Frome Museum.
11. Somerset Record Office, Taunton
12. Somersetshire Coal Canal Lock Fund Report, 1 March 1806.
13. W. Phelps, *The History and Antiquities of Somersetshire*, 1836, Vol 1, p 57.
14. *The New Bath Directory, Corrected to May, 1812.*
15. Worcester & Birmingham Canal Minute Book, 1 February 1809.
16. *An Authentic Description of the Kennet & Avon Canal*, 1811.
17. *A Topographical and historical description of the County of Somerset*, being Part 3 of Vol 10 of the *Beauties of England and Wales* series edited by John Britton and E. W. Brayley, 1813.
18. *The History of Wincanton*, op cit, p 216.
19. For the evolution of the steam locomotive prior to 1825, see *Archive Teaching Unit No. 3: Railway in the Making*, 1969, compiled by R. M. Gard and J. R. Hartley for the University of Newcastle-upon-Tyne Department of Education.

20 *Sherborne Mercury*, 29 August 1825.
21. Ibid.

NOTES TO CHAPTER 6 (*pages* 64–71)

1. For the history of the English & Bristol Channels Ship Canal, see Charles Hadfield, *The Canals of South West England*, 1967, pp 41–5.
2. 6 Geo IV, c 199.
3. *The Canals of South West England*, op cit, p 38.
4. Ibid, p 84.
5. For a full history of the Basingstoke Canal, see P. A. L. Vine, *London's Lost Route to Basingstoke*, 1969.
6. *Remarks on a letter from Mr. Page* by 'A Friend of the People', 1810.
7. *Sherborne Mercury*, 19 September 1825.
8. Ibid.
9. Ibid, 17 October 1825.
10. Ibid, 31 October 1825.
11. *The Dorset and Somerset Canal Navigation*, op cit.
12. *Sherborne Mercury*, 31 October 1825.
13. Ibid, 7 November 1825.
14. Ibid.
15. Ibid.

NOTES TO CHAPTER 7 (*pages* 72–9)

1. *Sherborne Mercury*, 14 November 1825.
2. *Bath Herald*, 12 November 1825.
3. *Sherborne Mercury*, 14 November 1825.
4. Ibid.
5. Ibid.
6. Ibid, 21 November 1825.
7. Ibid, 5 December 1825.
8. Ibid.
9. Ibid.
10 *Bath Herald*, 31 December 1825.
11. *Sherborne Mercury*, 26 December 1825.
12. Ibid, 30 January 1826.
13. *Bath Chronicle*, 9 February 1826.
14. *Sherborne Mercury*, 30 January 1826.
15. Ibid, 13 February 1826.
16. *Exeter Flying Post*, 2 February 1826.
17. *Bath Chronicle*, 9 February 1826.

NOTES TO EPILOGUE (*pages* 80–1)

1. Robin Atthill, *Old Mendip*, 1964, p 171.
2. Lord Hylton, *Notes on the History of the Parish of Kilmersdon*, 1910, pp 116–17.
3. Letter from Registrar of Deeds & Records, BTHR.
4. Somerset Record Office, Taunton.

F

5. *Notes on the History of the Parish of Kilmersdon*, op cit, pp 116–17.
6. I am grateful to Robin Atthill for this information.
7. *The Dorset and Somerset Canal Navigation*, op cit.

Note on Sources

SUCH records as remain of the Dorset & Somerset Canal are distributed amongst several different authorities, though a central collection of material concerned with this canal is being gathered together at Bath Reference Library, Queen Square. This collection will, of necessity, be in the form of photo copies of the original documents, the latter continuing to be held by the respective bodies as detailed below:

Authority	*Records*
Dorset Record Office, Dorchester	Deposited plans. Pamphlet, *The Dorset and Somerset Canal Navigation*. Letter relating to subscriptions, 1797. Plan showing new cut at Fiddleford Water. Share tickets.
House of Lords Record Office, London	Acts of Parliament relating to canal, 1796 & 1803. Deposited plans and list of subscribers. Estimates of cost of construction, 1796.
Somerset Record Office, Taunton	Deposited plans. Share tickets.
British Transport Historical Records, London	Pamphlet, *The Dorset and Somerset Canal Navigation*.

A copy of Mr R. K. Bluhm's unpublished thesis *A Bibliography of the Somerset Coalfield* is lodged at the Library Association Library, 7 Ridgmount Street, London, WC1. This thesis contains many references to the canal, as also do the files of the local newspapers, particularly the *Sherborne Mercury*, *Felix Farley's Bristol Journal* and *Bath Chronicle*.

Author's Notes and Acknowledgements

ONE result of decimalisation has been that the *s* and *d* now only refer to historic sums of money. In consequence I have rounded off all large amounts to the nearer £. In all other cases, except within a quotation, the decimal equivalent is given in brackets after the sum mentioned.

The history of the Dorset & Somerset Canal could not have been written without the help and encouragement of the many good friends and organisations listed below and, in expressing my gratitude for their kindness, I am no less grateful to anyone else whose name I may have inadvertently omitted.

My thanks go to the archivists and staff of Bristol Archives Office; British Transport Historical Records; the County Record Offices of Dorset, Somerset and Wiltshire; the Duchy of Cornwall Office; the House of Lords Record Office; the superintendents and staff of the British Museum Reading Room and Newspaper Library; and to the Library Association Library.

I am also indebted to the librarians and staff of Bath Municipal Libraries, especially the director, Mr Peter Pagan, who has kindly written the foreword to this book, and Mr V. J. Kite, who has cheerfully answered my many tiresome queries; Mr H. E. Radford of Bournemouth Central Library; Bristol Central Library; Bruton Library; Mr H. F. V. Johnstone of Poole Central Library; Mr D. C. Totterdell of Street Library;

Miss M. Jupe of Swanage Library; and Mrs G. Norman of Wincanton Library.

The editor of the *Western Gazette*, Mr J. N. Goodchild, kindly allowed me to consult the files of the *Sherborne Mercury*. Other valuable information has been supplied by the Duchy of Cornwall Office; the Earl of Oxford; Miss J. M. R. Campbell and Mr F. N. James of the National Westminster Bank; Mr F. R. Shute, Town Clerk of Wareham; Mr J. N. Widdup, Clerk of the Council, Wincanton; and Messrs C. G. Down, G. W. Quartley, A. P. Voce and C. P. Weaver.

I express my grateful thanks to the following individuals and organisations who have kindly allowed me to reproduce their copyright photographs and illustrations: pages 33 (above and below), 34 (above and below) and 51 (above and below), Mr K. F. Marchant; page 52, Dorset Record Office; Fig 4 is based on a photograph by Mrs E. L. Green-Armytage; Fig 5, Duchy of Cornwall Office; Fig 6, Somerset Record Office; Fig 7, the Earl of Oxford and Asquith (from the Horner MSS); and Map 3, Mr R. A. Atthill.

Map 1 is based on a map of the D & S which appeared in *A Topographical and historical description of the County of Somerset*, 1813, and Map 2 on the first edition of the one inch Ordnance Survey map of Eastern Mendip, 1817.

It would have been impossible to carry out the field research without the help of my good friend, Bill Beaven, who has transported me in his car throughout the Mendip countryside between Bath and Bruton. I am equally grateful to both Robin Atthill and Gerald Quartley for their guidance on many of these field expeditions to view the remains of the canal.

Both Robin Atthill and Charles Hadfield deserve a special word of thanks for stimulating my interest in the canal by making available to me their files of information about the D & S. They have also read through the draft of this book and have made many constructive suggestions about it, as also has my mother-in-law.

Lastly, but by no means least, I owe far more than words can express to my wife for her help, patience and encouragement in the preparation of this book. She has prepared Figs 2, 3 and 4, and the roughs for Maps 1 and 2.

The Remains of the Canal

The following particulars are included as a guide for anyone wishing to view the remains of the canal. It is emphasised that several of these sites are on private property and that prior permission to view should be obtained from the owners concerned.

Nearly 168 years have passed since work stopped on the construction of the Dorset & Somerset Canal and, despite the depredations of the bulldozer in recent years, it is remarkable how much of it still remains.

The terminal basin at Stratton Common is now hard to distinguish owing to the levelling of the land, and the first notable sign of the canal is a bridge at Edford (ST 668489), built to carry the old packhorse road from the Stratton coalpits. It straddles a depression in the ground that once was the bed of the D & S. About half a mile east of this bridge is one of the best-preserved sections of the canal from ST 677487 to ST 681484. Here there is a culvert carrying a stream under the firmly made embankment, and the scene from the towpath is that of a canal well filled with water.

There is a fine two-arched aqueduct at Coleford (ST 685488), built to span the valley formed by a tributary of the Emborough stream. Known locally as 'Hucky Duck', the aqueduct's appearance has been spoilt in recent years by the removal of the 4ft to 6ft high parapet that once surmounted the structure. Apparently an enterprising local man sold the parapet in small quantities to local builders.

To the east of the Wesleyan chapel at Coleford (ST 687489) is another well-preserved stretch of the canal, extending for about half a mile towards Goodeaves. It begins in a cutting by the chapel and within a few hundred yards is carried on an embankment across a small valley. It continues to follow the 425ft contour line, ending in a cutting that has been filled in at one end by a rubbish tip. At one time the cutting continued to the mouth of Goodeaves tunnel, but this has long since been covered over by mounds of refuse, scrap iron, old cars, etc. The northernmost end of the tunnel, too, is obscured by a rubbish tip, but the course of the canal can be traced from ST 694494 northwards. Leaving a cutting, it ran alongside the bend in the Highbury to Newbury road, passing the front of the cottages at ST 693497 and then followed the route of the now disused railway line from the Newbury and Mackintosh collieries. This railway line was built on the bed of the canal and so no traces remain until Vobster Cross is neared, where there is a half-mile stretch intact, complete with towing path. Strangely, this is the only section of the D & S that appears on the current one inch edition of the Ordnance Survey map. At ST 707494 the original canal bridge can be seen underneath the now busy Mells to Highbury road.

The railway line and canal run close to each other for much of the way from Mells Road station to Frome. At Barrow hill (ST 735505) is the site of James Fussell's 'balance lock'. There is very little of the masonry remaining and it is now hard to visualise that this was once the site of three successful experiments in raising and lowering boats between the two levels.

Within a short distance all trace of the canal bed is lost, and about a quarter-mile has to be traversed before the line re-appears. This leads to the topmost of four unfinished balance locks, and close by the top lock is the remains of a small kiln, no doubt used in conjunction with the stone quarry to be found close by. The two middle locks (ST 747500) are in the best condition of the four, the third from bottom showing traces

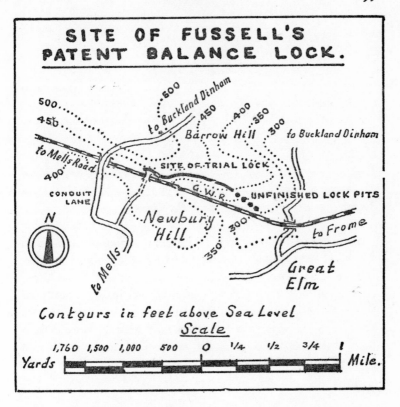

SITE OF FUSSELL'S
PATENT BALANCE LOCK.

Contours in feet above Sea Level
Scale
Yards   Mile.

of the middle buttress that was once intended to separate the
twin lock chambers.

It is almost 1 mile from this point to the next major engineering work at Murtry aqueduct (ST 762498). This is a three-
arched aqueduct built to span the stream from Emborough
which, augmented by several other brooks, forms the appearance of a lively river at this point. A further half-mile leads to
the last of the D & S—the 'Roman wall', a long stretch of stone
built embankment to the north of Whatcombe Farm (ST
771494), popularly attributed to the Romans, yet built by canal
contractors before the money ran out in 1803.

The Cost of the Canal

The following details are reproduced from the estimates produced for the House of Lords Select Committee in 1796, at the time that the D&S Bill was progressing through Parliament.

Estimate of the proposed Dorset and Somerset Canal from the Road near Gains Cross in the parish of Shillingston Okeford in the County of Dorset to the Kennet and Avon Canal near Widbrook in the parish of Bradford in the County of Wilts. With a branch from the same Canal near the Town of Frome, to the Southern Collieries near Mendip at or near a place called Nettlebridge in the parish of Midsummer Norton in the County of Somerset.

Miles		*£*
12	Of digging, embanking, lining, Puddling, forming and Gravelling Towing Paths &c. from the Road near Gains Cross aforesaid to the Southerly end of Wincanton Level near Stalbridge . . .	7,926
	Extra Cutting and Embanking on the above Length . . .	5,504
	56 Ft. of Lockage Do. . . .	3,920
	Bridges, Culverts, &c. for 12 miles . . .	3,000
	Land for Do. length of Canal 12 miles suppose 6 Acres per Mile is 72 Acres . . .	2,880
7¾	of digging, embanking, lining, puddling &c. from thence to Shatterwell Bridge at Wincanton . . .	5,152
	Extra Work in Do. Length . . .	253
	Bridges &c. for 7¾ miles . . .	1,937
	Land for 7¾ Miles suppose 6 Acres per Mile suppose 46½ Acres . . .	2,325

Miles   £

2¼   of digging &c. &c. from Shatterwell Bridge
aforesaid to the Northerly End of the head or Summit Level in Mr. Webb's Crockley Heys . . .   1,480

     Extra Cutting in the above Length in Lockpits
&c. . . .   428

     94½ Ft. of Lockage upon the above length by
Caissons . . .   2,833

10½   of digging &c. &c. from the Southerly end aforesaid to the Northerly end of the Summit Level in
Dirly Farm near Trudoxell (exclusive of the Tunnel) . . .   7,102

½   of Tunnel under the Earl of Ilchester's Coach
Road near Brewham . . .   10,090

     Extra Cutting at each end of the Tunnel, with an
embankment at Brewham and deep Cutting at
Billericay &c. &c. . . .   14,423

5¼   of digging &c. &c. from the Northerly End of the
Summit Level to the Point of Junction with the
Branch to Coal Works in William Davis's Field be-
low Frome . . .   3,546

     extra Cutting or digging in the Lock Pits &c. &c.
embanking upon the said Length . . .   2,723

     115¼ Ft. of Lockage (downward) in the above
length by Caissons . . .   3,463

9¼   of digging &c. &c. from the junction with the
Coal Branch aforesaid to the junction with the
Kennet and Avon Canal near Widbrook . . .   6,034

     Extra Cutting and embanking upon the said
Length . . .   2,256

     102½ Ft. of Lockage from Frome to the Junction
with the Kennet & Avon near Widbrook by Caissons . . .   3,074

     Road and other Bridges for 28 Miles in Length
suppose . . .   7,000

     Land for 28 Miles in length suppose 6 Acres per
Mile is 168 Acres at . . .   7,560

     Temporary Damages, Accidents, Engines, Super-
intendants &c. suppose 10 per cent upon the
whole . . .   10,491

     ————

     115,400

BRANCH TO COAL WORKS

Miles		*£*
6¼	of digging, embanking, lining, puddling, forming and gravelling Towing Paths from the point of Junction in Wm. Davis's Field near Frome to the Road to Vobster at Torr . . .	4,961
	To an Aqueduct and Embankment at Murtry Mill . . .	318
	To extra cutting in the Lockpits &c. from thence to the Road to Vobster near the Torr . . .	706
	To extra Work in the Brows from Frome to Murtry Mill . . .	150
	207¾ Ft. of Lockage by Caissons . . .	6,240
	To Road and Occupation Bridges, Culverts &c. for 6¼ miles . . .	1,562
	Land for 6¼ Miles suppose 6 Acres per Mile 37½ Acres at . . .	1,868
4¾	of digging, embanking &c. &c. from the Torr to Nettlebridge . . .	3,844
	extra Cutting and Embanking on the above Length . . .	2,914
	To Tunnelling 162 Yards in Length . . .	1,134
	Extra Cutting in the 7 Lockpits &c. . . .	200
	56½ Ft. of Lockage by Caisson . . .	1,695
	Road for Occupation Bridges for 4¾ Miles . . .	1,219
	Land for 4⅞ Miles suppose 7 Acres per Mile suppose 34 Acres . . .	1,020
	Temporary Damages, Accidents, Engines, Superintendants, &c. suppose 10 per cent . . .	2,783
		————
		30,584

APPENDIX 3

Fussell's Invention

In Patent No 2284 of 24 December 1798, James Fussell describes his invention of 'A Machine or Balance Lock for Raising Boats from a Lower Level of a Canal to an Upper, or Lowering the same from an Upper to a Lower Level of a Canal'. The specification is reproduced below.

The nature and method of my invention is by a perpendicular lift, by balance lock, or machine with wheels, chains, balances, screws, vessels, or receptacles, levers, shafts and rack wheels of a particular construction as herein-after described.

First, suppose a particular rise or fall, as, for instance, from forty to fifty feet, which is about equal to the rise or fall of six or eight common locks, and which I propose to overcome without the loss of water, to construct which your canal should be brought to a quick or steep descent of a hill, and if the lift intended is not above forty or fifty feet this lock may be built open at the end next to the lower level, with two side walls, and one end wall to the upper level, and also a partition wall to divide the said lock into two equal parts, which may be called lock pits, and is herein-after more fully described; but if requisite or convenient to have a very deep lift, for instance, one hundred feet or more, it will be necessary to wall the said lock pits both sides and ends, and to have a short tunnel from the lower level to the bottom of the lock pits. The lock pits must be built long and wide enough for the receptacles which are intended to convey the boats or barges up or down from one level to another (which receptacles must be two in number and made exactly of the same dimensions), with a partition wall or framing in the middle, of the same thickness as the width of the aperture or lock pit, and built either of brick, stone, or timber; on this partition is to be placed or fixed a shaft of sufficient strength, upon each of which a wheel is to be fixed of greater diameter by two or more inches than the thickness of the said wall or partition, so that the chain which works over the said wheels shall hang or work clear of the partition wall in descending or ascending. Now the receptacles are two open boxes or cisterns of sufficient length, and suitable to receive the boats or barges intended for the trade, about six feet width inside and from three to six feet deep, made of wood, iron, or any other metal, so as to be made water-tight; under each of these receptacles is fixed a very strong framing of oak timber, secured with braces and bolts of iron, &c., and of dimensions and strength fit to support two wheels of equal diameter with those on the shaft above described; and placed at similar distances upon each corner of the upper part of the receptacles, and also at the lower corners of the framing are placed small iron wheels or rollers which run in grooves of iron fixed upon timbers placed in the wall for that purpose, which guide the receptacles and keep them horizontal. To regulate the motion and fix it in any position there is a tooth wheel fixed on one of the wheels of the shaft aforesaid, which works into a pinion fixed on a small shaft or spindle, with a fly and break wheel thereon. Now the two receptacles and frames underneath must be made exactly of the same dimensions in every respect so as to balance each other, and, as they are to be filled with water of an equal depth, will be of equal weights; and in order to preserve a balance on the works it will be necessary to fix a balance chain to the bottom of each receptacle, of equal weight per foot or yard with the chain that works the machine, which will alternatively counterpoise each other in ascending or descending. Now there are two chains made of wrought or cast iron, or other metal, of sufficient length according to the height of the fall, and of strength more than adequate to the weight to be raised or let down; these chains are placed over the two wheels of the shaft which rests upon the wall or partition between the lock pits as before described, and then carried under the two wheels (which are also fixed upon each end of a shaft which works within the framing under each of the said receptacles), and the ends of the said chains are then fastened or fixed with screws, or by any other method, at the top of the side wall (or framing) of each lock pit. At each end of either of the receptacles as aforesaid is placed hatches hung up by chains, ropes, or otherwise balances, with weights, or raised and lowered with rack wheels, when it is intended to receive or discharge a boat or barge, or other vessel as aforesaid. The hatch is to be let down into a groove or case fixed at each end of the two receptacles till the top part of the hatch is level with the bottom of the receptacles, which will then admit the boat or barge to float over it. The upper and lower levels or canals must also be divided into two mouths, troughs, or apertures, each to fix the ends of the receptacles, to make the mouths of the canal and that of the receptacles water-tight. The ends of the receptacles which fix to the mouths of the upper level must be a little wider than the mouth of the canal, in order to clip tight, and the ends which fit to the lower levels must be a little less than the mouth of the canal, so as it sinks down to the mouth of the lower canal it clips the ends of the receptacles sufficiently long to make it water-tight, when a small wadding of leather or cloth is fixed between the joints; or it may be made water-tight by having the ends of the receptacles brought exactly opposite to the mouths of the canal, and as near as can be to each other without touching, when a short purchase may be applied with a lever, and small weight let drop by a cord, or any other method which will press it against the mouth of the canal with a sufficient force to make it water-tight. Now, suppose you have raised one boat and lowered down another, the first thing to be done is to touch the break wheel and fix the receptacle tight up to the mouth of the canal, then to move a valve which is in the door at the mouth or entrance of the canal, which admits the water out of the canal into a small space between the door of the canal and the hatch of the receptacle, when the hatch in the receptacle is to be sunk and the stop gate or door of the canal to be opened, by which means the water in the canal and the water of the receptacles will be united, and the boat will be floated out of the upper and lower receptacles and others floated in: when done, the door is to be shut and the hatch drawn up, when a valve is to be opened in the bottom of the space between the door and hatch, by which means the water is conveyed by a pipe into a small reservoir or trough fixed under the bottom of the receptacle which makes the receptacle at the higher end or level of greater weight than the lower; but if the small quantity of water between the hatch and door be not sufficient to overbalance it more may be taken out of the upper level, which water, when it acts to the bottom or lower level, discharges itself by a plug or valve, and carried off by means of culvert or otherwise. This machine or balance lock is not confined to a perpendicular lift; for instance, if the hill to descend should be found of a very hard rock, it will be less expensive to adapt an inclined plane in the following manner: First, two railways must be placed side by side from the upper to the lower level, and between those a space of seven or eight feet, more or less, as may be most convenient; at the top of this space or head of the upper level must be fixed a strong wheel, with the same inclination as the railways; over this wheel is a strong chain fastened to each receptacle, and at the bottom of those receptacles must be a strong framing of wood, in which frame will be four or more wheels of different dimensions, to keep the receptacles always in a horizontal position, to join the mouths or apertures of the canal at the upper and lower levels, when similar methods must be used to make them watertight, and transfer the boats as described in the perpendicular lift. This machine or balance lock may also be applied to various other useful purposes.

JAMES FUSSELL

APPENDIX 4

Bye-Laws

THE enabling Act of 1796 (36 Geo III, c 47) made provision for 'Rules, Bye Laws, and Orders' for the 'good Government' of the Canal. No copies of any such bye-laws have been traced, though certain sections of the Act do give a good idea of the type of regulation proposed:

Section XCIX (Collection of tolls)

. . . That the Master, Owner, or Manager, or Person having the Care of every Boat, Barge, or other Vessel, navigating upon the said Canal or Branch, shall give an exact and true Account in Writing, signed by him or them, to the Collector of the said Rates, at the Place or Places where he or they shall attend for that Purpose, of the Quantity, Quality, and Weight, of the Goods, Wares, and Merchandize, which shall be in or belong to such Boat, Barge, or other Vessel, from whence brought, and where the same are intended to be landed; and if the Goods contained in such Boat, Barge, or other Vessel, shall be liable to the Payment of different Rates, then such Master, Owner, or Persons, shall specify the Quantities liable to the Payment of each Rate; and in case any such Person shall neglect or refuse to give such Account, or to produce his Bill of Lading to any such Collector demanding the same, or shall give a false Account, or shall deliver any Part of his Lading or Goods at any other Place than what is or are mentioned in such Account, with Intent to avoid Payment of the said Rates, or any Part thereof, he shall forfeit and pay the Sum of Five Pounds for every such Offence over and above the respective Rates directed to be paid for the same by virtue thereof.

Section CVI (Passage through locks)

... That no Boatman or other Person navigating or having the Care of any Boat, Barge, or other Vessel, which shall pass through any lock to be made upon the said Canal or Branch, shall suffer the Water to remain in such Lock longer than is necessary for his Boat, Barge, or other Vessel to pass through the same; and that every such Boatman or other Person as aforesaid, in going down the said Canal, or Branch, from the respective Head Levels thereof, shall, previously to his bringing the Boat, Barge, or other Vessel, into any Lock, shut the lower Gates of such Lock and the Sluices thereto belonging, before he shall draw the Sluices of the upper Gates thereof; and after he shall have brought his Boat, Barge, or other Vessel into the said Lock, he shall then shut the upper Gates thereof, and the sluices thereto belonging, before he shall draw the Sluices of the lower Gates thereof; and in going up the said Canal or Branch towards the respective Head Levels thereof, such Boatman or other Person shall, as soon as he shall have passed with his Boat, Barge, or other Vessel out of the said Lock, shut the upper Gates thereof and the Sluices thereto belonging, and afterwards draw the Sluices of the lower Gates thereof, unless there shall be then a Boat, Barge, or other Vessel, in Sight from the said Lock, coming down the said Canal, or Branch, in which case the lower Gates of the said Lock, and the Sluices thereof, shall be left shut, and the upper Gates shall be left open; and at all Times the Vessels going up the said Canal and Cut respectively, if within sight from any Vessel coming down, and at a Distance not exceeding Three hundred Yards below any Lock, shall pass through such Lock before the Vessel coming down, and then the Vessel above such Lock shall come down; and if there shall be no more Vessels than one below and above any Lock at the same Time, within the Distance aforesaid, at which Distance a Post or Mark shall be set up or made for ascertaining the same, such Vessels shall go up and come down through such Lock by Turns as aforesaid, until the Vessels going up and coming down shall have passed the same, in order that one Lock full of Water may serve two Vessels; and that every Person who shall offend in any of these Particulars, shall for every such Offence forfeit a Sum not exceeding Five Pounds, nor less than Twenty Shillings.

Section CVIII (Lock keepers not to give preference)

... That if any Lock Keeper, Wharfinger, or other Servant belonging to the said Company of Proprietors, shall give any Preference, or shew Partiality to any Boat, Barge, or other Vessel, in passing through any Lock upon the said intended Canal, or Branch, or in loading or unloading any Goods or other Things at any of the Wharfs, Warehouses, Weigh Beams, Cranes, and other Machines, belonging to the said Company of Proprietors, every Person so offending shall forfeit and pay the Sum of Twenty Shillings to the Informer.

Section CIX (Owners names to be on boats)

... That every Owner, Master, or Person, having the Rule or Command of any Boat, Barge, or other Vessel, passing upon the said intended Canal, or Branch, shall cause his or her Name and Place of Abode, and the Number of his or her Boat, Barge, or other Vessel, to be entered with the Clerk to the said Company of Proprietors, and shall also cause such Name and Number to be painted in large White Capital Letters and Figures of the Length of Four Inches at the least, on a Black Ground, and of a proportionable Breadth, on the Outside of the Head or Stern of every such Boat, Barge, or other Vessel, higher than the Place to which the same shall sink into the Water when full laden; and also shall, and is hereby required, to fix on each Side thereof respectively, correct Indexes of Copper, Lead, or other Metal, of such graduated Dimensions, and of such convenient Heights, and under such Regulations as the said Company of Proprietors shall from Time to Time direct, so that the true Weight of the Lading on board may at all Times be thereby ascertained and shewn, and shall permit and suffer every such Boat, Barge, or other Vessel to be gauged or measured at the Expence of the said Company of Proprietors, whenever it shall be required by them or any Person or Persons appointed for that Purpose, provided that no such Boat, Barge, or other Vessel, shall be gauged or measured more than Four Times in any one Year; and every Owner, Master, or other Person having the Rule or Command of any Boat, Barge, or other Vessel, who shall navigate the same upon the said intended Canal, or Branch, without having such Name, Figures, and Index thereon, as are herein-before directed, or shall fix any

false Name, Figures, or Index, or who shall refuse to permit and
suffer the same to be gauged and measured, shall, for every such
Offence, forfeit and pay any Sum not exceeding Five Pounds.

Section CX (Owners liability)

. . . That the Master or Owner of any Boat, Barge, or other
Vessel, navigating upon the said intended Canal, or Branch,
shall be, and is hereby made answerable for any Damage, Spoil,
or Mischief, that shall be done by his Boat, Barge, or other
Vessel, or any of the Boatmen, Watermen, or others belonging
to, or employed in or about the same respectively, unto any
of the Bridges, Weirs, Locks, Banks, Dams, Engines, or other
Works, in, upon, or belonging to the said intended Canal or
Branch, or any of the Trenches, Tunnels, Aqueducts, Sluices
and Passages, to be made as aforesaid, or by loading or unloading any Boat, Barge, or other Vessel, and for any Trespass
or Damage that shall or may be done to the Owners or Occupiers of any Buildings, Erections, Lands, Tenements, or other
Property adjoining or lying near to the same, or any of them,
or any other Trespass whatsoever, contrary to the several
Directions and Restrictions in this Act contained, or any of
them; and the said Master or Owner of such Boat, Barge, or
other Vessel, shall, for every such Damage, upon Conviction of
such Person or Persons before any Justice of the Peace for the
County or Place where any such Offence shall be committed,
either by the Confession of the Party or Parties offending, or
upon the Oath or Oaths of One or more credible Witness or
Witnesses (which Oath or Oaths such Justice is hereby empowered and required to adminster), pay to the Person or
Persons injured, the Damages to be ascertained by such Justice,
provided such Damages do not exceed the Sum of Five Pounds,
and also shall, over and above such Damages, forfeit and pay to
the Informer any Sum not exceeding Twenty Shillings, and all
Costs, Charges, and Expenses, attending such Conviction;
which Damages, Fines, Penalties, and Costs, shall be levied by
Distress and Sale of the Goods and Chattels of the Master or
Owner or Owners of such Boat, Barge, or other Vessel, by
Warrant or Warrants under the Hand and Seal of such Justice,
and the Overplus (if any) after such Penalty, Fine, Damages,
and the Costs and Charges of such distress and Sale are deducted
shall be returned upon Demand to the Owner or Owners of

such Goods and Chattels; or if the said Damages shall exceed the said Sum of Five Pounds, then in such Case the Master, or Owner or Owners of such Boat, Barge, or other Vessel, shall and may be sued for the same in any Court of Record at *Westminster*; and if a Verdict pass against him, or Judgement be given against him upon Demurrer or by Default, the Plaintiff in such Case shall recover his Damages thereby sustained with full Costs of Suit.

Section CXVI (Only approved boats to use Canal)

. . . That no Person whosoever shall pass with, or use upon the said Canal or Branch, any Boat, Barge, or other Vessel (except Pleasure Boats), without being liable to the Payment of the Rates herein directed and unless the same be constructed, formed, and made, agreeably to the Orders and Regulations of the said Company of Proprietors, upon Pain of forfeiting for every such Offence any Sum not exceeding Twenty Pounds, nor less than Five Pounds; and a Table of the Rates and Tolls to be taken by virtue hereof shall be stuck upon every House erected for the Residence of the Collectors of the said Rates and Tolls.

Section CXVII (Opening of drawbridges)

. . . That if any Swivel Bridge or Draw Bridge shall be laid over or across the said Canal or Branch, Trenches or Passages for Water, to be made by virtue of this Act, all and every Person or Persons opening any such Draw Bridge, or Swivel Bridge for the Passage of any Boat, Barge, or other Vessel, shall from Time to Time, as soon as such Boat, Barge, or other Vessel shall have passed such Bridge, shut and fasten the same; and that every Person neglecting so to do shall forfeit and pay, for every such Offence, a Sum not exceeding Five Pounds; and in case any such Bridge shall be left open longer than necessary for the Passage of any Boat, Barge, or other Vessel as aforesaid, through the Neglect or Carelessness of any Person belonging to any such Boat, Barge, or Vessel, then the Master or Owner of such Boat, Barge, or other Vessel, shall forfeit and pay for every such Offence any Sum not exceeding Five Pounds; and if any Person or Persons shall wilfully open any such Draw Bridge or Swivel Bridge, when no Vessel is to pass through the same, so as to interrupt the free Passage for Travellers, Cattle, or Carriages,

every Person so offending shall for every such Offence forfeit
and pay any Sum not exceeding Five Pounds; all which said
Penalties or Forfeitures shall go and be applied, One Moiety
to the Informer, and the other Moiety to the Poor of the Town-
ship or Parish where the Offence shall be committed.

Section CXXV (Goods to be unloaded at a public wharf)

... That if any Person (except as herein mentioned) navigating
or working, or employed in navigating or working, any Boat,
Barge, or other Vessel upon the said Canal or Branch, shall
load or take into, or shall unload or take out of, any such
Boat, Barge, or other Vessel, any Goods, Wares, Merchandize, or
Things whatsoever, liable to the Payment of any of the Rates
herein-before mentioned, at any other Place or Places than at
the Wharfs or Quays, upon or belonging to the said Canal or
Branch respectively, without having first obtained the Consent
in Writing for that Purpose of the said Company of Proprietors,
or their Agent or Collector of the said Rates; every such Person
shall, for every such Offence, forfeit any Sum not exceeding
Twenty Pounds.

Section CXXVII (Regulations for vessels passing on the canal)

... That all Boats, Barges, or other Vessels navigated upon the
said Canal or Branch, shall, upon meeting any other Boat,
Barge, or Vessel, stop at or go back to, and lie in the Places to
be provided for that Purpose as aforesaid, in such Manner as
the said Company of Proprietors, or the said Committee, shall
from Time to Time direct and appoint; and it shall be lawful
for the said Company of Proprietors from Time to Time to
make such Rules and Regulations as they shall think proper, for
or relating to the passing of any Lock, or any Inclined Plane, or
other Substitute for a Lock, to be made by virtue of this Act,
with any Boats, Barges, or other Vessels; and all such Rules
and Regulations shall be binding upon, and be conformed to by
the Owners or Persons having the Care or Conduct of such
Boats, Barges, or other Vessels, upon Pain of forfeiting a Sum
not exceeding Five Pounds for every Default; and if any Boat,
Barge, or other Vessel shall be placed or suffered to remain in
any Part of the said Canal or Branch, so as to obstruct the Navigation thereof, and the Owner or Person having the Care of
such Boat, Barge, or other Vessel, shall not immediately, upon

Request made, remove such Boat, Barge, or other Vessel, he shall for every such Offence forfeit any Sum not exceeding Ten Shillings for every Hour such Obstruction shall continue after the making of such Request; and it shall be lawful for any Agent or Officer belonging to the said Company of Proprietors, to cause any such Boat, Barge, or other Vessel to be unloaded, (if necessary), and to be removed in such Manner as shall be proper for preventing such Obstruction, and to detain such Boat, Barge, or other Vessel, and the Loading thereof, or any Part of such Loading, until the Charges occasioned by such Removal are paid; and if any Boat, Barge, or other Vessel, shall be sunk in the said Navigation, or any Sluice, Tunnel, or Trench aforesaid, and the Owner or Person having the Care of such Boat, Barge, or other Vessel, shall not, without Loss of Time, weigh or draw up the same, it shall be lawful for the Agents or Servants of the said Company of Proprietors, or any of them, to cause such Boat, Barge, or other Vessel, to be weighed or drawn up, and to detain the same until Payment be made of all the Expences necessarily occasioned relating thereto.

Section CXXVIII (Persons obstructing the canal)

. . . That if any Person shall float any Timber upon the said Canal or Branch, or shall load any Boat, Barge, or other Vessel with Timber, or any other Thing, so that the same shall lie over the Side of any such Boat, Barge, or other Vessel, or shall overload any Boat, Barge, or other Vessel, navigating in or upon the said Canal or Branch, so as to obstruct the Passage of any Boat, Barge, or other Vessel, and shall not immediately, upon Notice given him for that Purpose, remove such Obstruction; or if any Person shall throw any Ballast, Gravel, Stones, or Rubbish, into any Part of the said Canal or Branch, or into any Trenches, Watercourses, Sluices, or other Works to be made by virtue of this Act; or if any Person or Persons shall wantonly, carelessly, or negligently open, or cause to be opened, any Lock Gate, or any Paddle, Valve, or Clough, belonging to any Lock, or any Cassoon or Machine to be erected on the said Canal or Branch, or shall leave open any Gate upon any Rail Way, or suffer any Boat, Barge, or other Vessel, to strike or run upon any of the said Bridges, Locks, or other Works, or shall wilfully flush or draw off the Water from any Part of the said Canal or Branch, or cause the same to be done, or shall leave any of the said Valves or Cloughs open, and running after any Boat, Barge, or other Vessel, shall have passed any such Lock, Cassoon, or other Machine, every Person so offending shall forfeit and pay for every such Offence any Sum not exceeding Five Pounds.

Section CXXIX (Persons wilfully destroying the works)

... That if any Person shall wilfully, maliciously, and to the Prejudice of the said Navigation, break, throw down, damage, or destroy, any Bank, or other Works to be erected and made by virtue of this Act, or cause the same to be done, every Person so offending, and being thereof lawfully convicted, shall be transported in like Manner as Felons are directed to be transported by the Laws and Statutes of this Realm, or otherwise the Court before whom such Person shall be convicted may, in Mitigation of such Punishment (if they think fit), award any such other Punishment as the Law directs in Cases of Petit Larcency; or otherwise every Person so offending, and being thereof lawfully convicted, on the Oath of One credible Witness, before One or more of His Majesty's Justices of the Peace for the County or Place where such Offence shall be committed, or the Offender shall be or reside, shall forfeit any Sum not less than Double nor more than Treble the Value of the Damage proved upon Oath to be done, at the Discretion of such Justice or Justices, such Penalty, together with reasonable Costs, to be levied by Distress and Sale of the Goods and Chattels of such Offender, rendering the Overplus (if any) to such Offender, or such Offender shall or may be committed to the Common Gaol for the County or Place where such Offence shall happen, for any Time not exceeding Three Calendar Months, at the Discretion of the Justice or Justices before whom such Offender shall be convicted.

Section CXXXVI (Unlawful fishing)

... That if any Person or Persons navigating or working, or being on board any Boat, Barge, or other Vessel upon the said Canal or Branch, (not being qualified by Law to kill Game), shall carry on board such Boat, Barge, or other Vessel, any Fishing Net, or other Engine so taking or destroying Fish or Game, every such Person shall, for every such Offence, forfeit and pay the Sum of Five Pounds; and in case any Master, or other Person, having the Command of any Boat, Barge, or other Vessel, passing upon the said Canal or Branch, shall wilfully suffer or permit any Person or Persons, not being qualified as aforesaid, to have or carry on board any Fishing Net or other Engine for taking or destroying Fish or Game, he shall, for every such Offence, forfeit the Sum of Five Pounds.

APPENDIX 5

Bibliography

BOOKS AND PAMPHLETS

Collinson, J. *History of Somerset*, 1791

Billingsley, John. *General View of the Agriculture of the County of Somerset*, 2nd ed, 1798

Phillips, John. *A General History of Inland Navigation, Foreign and Domestic; containing a Complete Account of the Canals already executed in England with Considerations on those Proposed*, 5th ed, 1805

An Authentic Description of the Kennet & Avon Canal, 1811

Rees' *Cyclopaedia*, 1819

Priestley, Joseph. *Historical Account of the Navigable Rivers, Canals, and Railways throughout Great Britain*, 1831

Phelps, W. *History and Antiquities of Somersetshire*, 1836

Sweetman, George. *The History of Wincanton*, 1903

Hylton, Lord. *Notes on the History of the Parish of Kilmersdon*, 1910

Atthill, Robin. *The Curious Past*, 1955.

Coysh, A. W., Mason, E. J. and Waite, V. *The Mendips*, 2nd ed, 1962

Atthill, Robin. *Old Mendip*, 1964

Hadfield, Charles. *The Canals of South West England*, 1967

Clew, Kenneth R. *The Kennet & Avon Canal*, 1968

Buchanan, Angus and Cossons, Neil. *The Industrial Archaeology of the Bristol Region*, 1969

Hadfield, Charles. *The Canals of South and South East England*, 1969

The First Edition of the One Inch Ordnance Survey—Sheet 76, Bath & Wells, reprinted 1969

Clew, Kenneth R. *The Somersetshire Coal Canal and Railways*, 1970

PERIODICALS

'The Somerset Coal Canals' by Atthill, Robin (*Country Life*, 6 April 1951)

'To Mendip for Coal' by Bulley, John A. (*Proceedings of the Somersetshire Archaeological & Natural History Society*, 1951–2)

'A Dynasty of Ironmasters' by Atthill, Robin (*Country Life*, 24 May 1962)

Index

Figures in **bold** type indicate plates in text